Chinese COOKING

CLB 1669
Published 1993 by CLB Publishing
Exclusively for Selecta Book Ltd, Devizes

Printed and bound in Spain by Graficromo S.A.
ISBN 1 85833 070 X

COMPILED AND EDITED BY
Delia Clarke

RECIPES WRITTEN BY
Lalita Ahmed, Judith Ferguson and Carolyn Garner

PHOTOGRAPHED BY
Peter Barry

DESIGNED BY
Philip Clucas MSIAD

Chinese COOKING

SELECT EDITIONS

CONTENTS

INTRODUCTION

As in many other countries so in China, the preparation and sharing of a meal are of great social and family importance. Mealtimes are when the whole family as well as friends gather together to share food and experiences, happiness and problems. To the Chinese, therefore, the meal is about more than just eating and satisfying a physical need, it is an integral and important part of their social life. Additionally, through cooking itself one demonstrates personal inventiveness and creativity, as well as one's cultural background, so cooking can always be seen as a pleasurable activity.

In Chinese cuisine, the preparation of the food is of paramount importance. Many dishes require very fine chopping and shredding of the various ingredients, and these are normally combined in a very orderly manner. Those ingredients which are not easily available in the Western world can generally be substituted. Many Chinese recipes, of course, feature ingredients so exotic that they cannot be found in the West, and these have been avoided in this book, whilst others have been included which, whilst not necessarily authentic, reflect a Chinese influence or means of preparation.

The main cooking technique used to produce good Chinese food is stir-frying. A wok is ideal, but a deep frying pan will serve the purpose almost as well. The traditional wok is made of a heavy-gauge carbon steel which conducts heat well, giving a quick high temperature. However, this medium will rust if not oiled and given proper care. Lengthy cooking in liquid may impart a metallic taste to the food, or may cause the discoloration of white liquids or food. Aluminium and stainless steel woks are also available and are a good choice, particularly if steaming, braising, boiling, or cooking for a long time. These woks need no seasoning, but do not heat as efficiently as carbon steel.

Stir-frying is a fuel and time saver and is unique to wok cooking, where small pieces of food are toss-cooked in minutes over intense heat in a very small amount of oil. The shape of the wok allows for tossing with abandon. Food is cooked in a matter of minutes and the flavours and juices remain sealed in, resulting in succulent meat, poultry and seafood, and tender and crisp vegetables. Nutritional values are retained, as are the fresh, bright colours of the vegetables.

Stir-frying requires good temperature control, and this is easily learnt with practice. The wok or pan should be heated, then the temperature reduced before adding the oil. If the utensil is too hot the oil will burn, giving a charred, oily taste to the food, which may burn, too. The heat should be progressively raised for the addition of other ingredients. All ingredients should be prepared and at hand before beginning to cook, and this includes any sauces or seasonings. Meat and poultry should be very thinly and evenly sliced, and ingredients that take the longest time to cook should be put into the wok first. Add small amounts of food at a time, in batches if necessary. Once cooked, the food must be served and eaten immediately.

Chinese food incorporates six basic flavours: sweet, sour, salty, spicy, pungent and hot. The use of these flavours and their respective proportions must be well balanced. Flavouring is always supplemented by ready-prepared sauces, the most essential of which is soy sauce. Others commonly used are plum and oyster sauces.

As in so much that is Oriental, presentation is every bit as important as the preparation. After all, what appeals to the eye also appeals to the mind, and thence to the heart and stomach. A slice of cleverly carved carrot, a thin sliver of tomato and cleverly arranged parsley or coriander can add that all-important dash of colour.

Garnishes for Chinese dishes tend to be very simple. The following two are quite easy to create, and can be prepared in advance:

Chilli Flowers Choose small red or green chilli peppers. Cut into thin strips, lengthways, to within ½-1 inch of the stem. Keep the stem end intact and carefully remove the seeds and core. Place in iced water for several hours or overnight until the 'petals' open up. Eat at your own risk!

Spring Onion Brushes Trim the onions into 3-4-inch lengths. Cut the greener end into thin strips and leave the white "bulb" end intact. Alternatively, cut both ends into thin strips, leaving ½ inch of the middle intact. Soak as for chilli flowers.

Although the microwave oven could be considered anathema to Chinese cooking, it adapts surprisingly well and many Chinese specialities are possible with a microwave oven. The usual cornflour-based Chinese sauces need more thickening because liquids evaporate less in a microwave, but otherwise they are easy to prepare. Stir-frying transfers successfully from the wok to the browning dish, and you can even achieve a stir-fried effect without one. The microwave section of this book features recipes prepared in a 700W oven. If using ovens of a different maximum power output, the following conversion can be used as a rough guide:
For **500W** ovens, add 40 seconds for each minute stated in the recipe.
For **600W** ovens, add 20 seconds for each minute stated in the recipe.
For **650W** ovens, you will only need to allow a slight increase in the cooking time over the 700W model.

Recipes featuring this symbol in the heading have been specially adapted for microwave preparation.

Chinese COOKING

SOUPS AND STARTERS

Chicken Corn Soup with Almonds

PREPARATION TIME: 15 minutes

MICROWAVE COOKING TIME: 5-8 minutes

SERVES: 4 people

2 225g (8oz) cans creamed corn
1150ml (2 pints) chicken stock
2 chicken breasts, finely chopped
30ml (2 tbsps) cornflour
30ml (2 tbsps) rice wine or dry sherry
60g (2oz) toasted almonds
Salt and pepper

Combine corn, stock and chicken in a large, deep bowl. Partially cover and cook 3-5 minutes or until chicken is nearly cooked. Combine rice wine and cornflour, and stir into the soup. Cook 2-3 minutes to allow cornflour to thicken and clear. Sprinkle with toasted almonds and serve.

Stuffed Mushrooms with Pork and Water Chestnuts

PREPARATION TIME: 30 minutes

MICROWAVE COOKING TIME: 4 minutes per batch

SERVES: 4 people

12 dried Chinese mushrooms
120g (4oz) minced pork
2 water chestnuts, finely chopped
1 stick celery, finely chopped
10ml (2 tsps) soy sauce
5ml (1 tsp) oyster sauce
Salt and pepper

GARNISH
4 spring onions, sliced

Soak the mushrooms in hot water for 30 minutes. Mix all the remaining ingredients. Drain the mushrooms and reserve 120ml (4 fl oz) of the soaking water. Pat the mushrooms dry on paper towels and cut off the stems. Combine

This page: Stuffed Mushrooms with Pork and Water Chestnuts. Facing page: Chicken Corn Soup with Almonds (top) and Soup of Mushrooms and Peas (page 10) (bottom).

remaining ingredients and fill the mushrooms with the pork mixture, smoothing out with a knife. Place the mushrooms in 1 layer in a shallow dish, stuffing-side up. Pour around the soaking water and cover the dish with pierced cling film. Cook on HIGH for 4 minutes. Baste occasionally with the mushroom liquid. Transfer the mushrooms to a serving dish and sprinkle with the onions. Serve hot.

Soup of Mushrooms and Peas

PREPARATION TIME: 15 minutes

MICROWAVE COOKING TIME: 10 minutes

SERVES: 4 people

12 dried Chinese mushrooms, soaked 30 minutes
120g (4oz) ham, shredded
1150ml (2 pints) light stock
15ml (1 tbsp) light soy sauce
225g (8oz) fresh peas
Salt and pepper

Remove the stems and slice the mushrooms finely. Combine with the remaining ingredients and cook 10 minutes on HIGH or until peas are just tender.

Hot and Sour Soup

PREPARATION TIME: 20 minutes

COOKING TIME: 7-8 minutes

SERVES: 6-8 people

1.5 litres (2½ pints) chicken stock
50g (2oz) pork, shredded, or cubed barbecued pork
50g (2oz) peeled shrimp
25g (1oz) bamboo shoots, sliced
2 cloud ear fungus, soaked in boiling water for 5 minutes and chopped
2-3 spring onions, chopped
Salt to taste
15ml (1 tbsp) sugar
2.5ml (½ tsp) monosodium glutamate (optional)
5ml (1 tsp) dark soy sauce
2.5ml (½ tsp) light soy sauce
22.5ml (1½ tbsp) malt vinegar
5ml (1 tsp) chilli oil or chilli sauce
1.25ml (¼ tsp) sesame oil
2.5ml (½ tsp) Shao Hsing wine (optional)
1 egg, well beaten
15ml (1 tbsp) cornflour or arrowroot
30ml (2 tbsps) water

Mix stock with pork, shrimp, and all the remaining ingredients except the well-beaten egg, cornflour and water. Simmer gently for 4-5 minutes. Remove from heat and add the egg, stirring gently, until the egg forms 'threads' in the soup. Blend the cornflour with the water and add to the soup. Simmer for 1 minute until the soup thickens. Serve immediately.

Chicken Noodle Soup

PREPARATION TIME: 10 minutes

COOKING TIME: 10-12 minutes

SERVES: 8 people

450g (1lb) Shanghai noodles, or very thin noodles
30ml (2 tbsps) oil
225g (8oz) cooked chicken, cubed
175g (6oz) Chinese white caggage or ordinary white cabbage, shredded
1½ litres (2½ pints) chicken stock

SEASONING
2.5ml (½ tsp) sugar
2.5ml (½ tsp) salt
10ml (2 tsps) Shao Hsing wine (optinal)
2.5ml (½ tsp) monosodium glutamate
10ml (2 tsps) light soy sauce

Add the noodles to a large pan of boiling water. Stir to loosen the bundles and boil for 4-5 minutes. (The noodles should be just tender but not overcooked.) Drain noodles well. Meanwhile, heat the oil in the wok and fry the chicken for 1-2 minutes. Remove the chicken and then fry the cabbage in the same oil for 2 minutes. Add the seasoning ingredients and stir-fry for 1 minute. Add the chicken and cook for a further 1-2 minutes until the cabbage is tender. Add the stock and bring to the boil. Divide noodles among 6-8 warm soup bowls and add the hot soup. Serve immediately.

Chinese Parsley and Fish Soup

PREPARATION TIME: 10 minutes

COOKING TIME: 7-8 minutes

SERVES: 6 people

450g (1lb) whitefish fillet, cut into 6 even-sized pieces
1 litre (1¾ pints) chicken stock
1cm (½ inch) fresh root ginger, peeled and thinly sliced
Salt to taste
Freshly ground black pepper to taste
Pinch monosodium glutamate (optional)
2 spring onions, finely chopped
2.5ml (½ tsp) arrowroot or cornflour
2 sprigs Chinese parsley, finely chopped
18–20 thin cucumber slices

Wash the fish in cold water and gently simmer in chicken stock for 2-3 minutes. Remove the fish pieces carefully. Add ginger, salt, pepper, monosodium glutamate and onion, and simmer the stock for 2-3 minutes. Strain. Dissolve arrowroot in 15ml (1 tbsp) of water or cold stock and add to the soup. Simmer for 2 minutes until the soup thickens. Add fish pieces and bring back to the boil. Serve in soup bowls, sprinkled with chopped parsley and cucumber slices.

Duck Soup

PREPARATION TIME: 10 minutes

COOKING TIME: 8 minutes

SERVES: 6 people

2 spring onions, finely chopped
15ml (1 tbsp) cooked oil, or standard cooking oil
2.5cm (1 inch) fresh root ginger, peeled and finely chopped
100g (4oz) cooked duck meat, chopped
100g (4oz) winter melon, thinly sliced
1.5 litres (2½ pints) chicken stock
Salt to taste

Facing page: Chicken Noodle Soup (top), Hot and Sour Soup (centre left) and Chinese Parsley and Fish Soup (bottom).

Pinch monosodium glutamate (optional)
15ml (1 tbsp) Shao Hsing wine or dry sherry (optional)
5ml (1 tsp) arrowroot or cornflour blended with 15ml (1 tbsp) stock
Freshly ground black pepper to taste

Fry spring onions in the oil for 1 minute. Add ginger and duck meat. Stir-fry for 1 minute. Add winter melon and stir-fry for a further 1-2 minutes and then add stock and the remaining ingredients. Gently simmer for 2-3 minutes until the soup becomes clear. Serve immediately.

Steamed Open Dumplings

PREPARATION TIME: 1 hour

COOKING TIME: 10-15 minutes

MAKES: 24 dumplings

FILLING
100g (4oz) peeled prawns, finely chopped
175g (6oz) pork or beef, minced
2 black mushrooms, soaked and finely chopped
Salt to taste
2.5ml (½ tsp) brown sugar

SEASONING
2.5ml (½ tsp) monosodium glutamate (optional)
15ml (1 tbsp) cornflour
5ml (1 tsp) dark soy sauce
5ml (1 tsp) light soy sauce
1.25ml (¼ tsp) freshly ground black pepper
15ml (1 tbsp) sesame oil
24 wonton wrappers

Mix together the minced pork, prawns, mushrooms, salt and sugar. Add the seasoning ingredients and mix well. Allow to stand for 30 minutes. Take each wonton wrapper (see recipe) and spoon a little filling in the centre. Fold up the edges around the filling but do not completely enclose it. (An open-ended dumpling is produced with the sides of the wrapper gathered around the filling.) Flatten the base by pressing it slighty so that it will stand upright in a steamer. Grease an ordinary steamer or a bamboo steamer and arrange the dumplings in it. Steam for 15-20 minutes. Serve hot with a dip.

Chicken and Mushroom Soup

PREPARATION TIME: 20 minutes

COOKING TIME: 6-8 minutes

SERVES: 6 people

100g (4oz) button mushrooms, sliced
50g (2oz) dried brown mushrooms, soaked and then sliced
50g (2oz) dried black mushrooms, soaked and then sliced
15ml (1 tbsp) oil
1.5 litres (2½ pints) chicken stock
100g (4oz) shredded cooked chicken
3 spring onions, finely chopped
1.25ml (¼ tsp) monosodium glutamate (optional)
Salt to taste
15ml (1 tbsp) light soy sauce
10ml (2 tsp) Shao Hsing wine (optional)
Pinch ground white pepper
5ml (1 tsp) cornflour or arrowroot blended with 15ml (1 tbsp) stock

Stir-fry the mushrooms in the oil for 2 minutes and then remove and set aside. Bring the stock to the boil in a large pan with the remaining ingredients, apart from the cornflour and mushrooms, and simmer for 3-4 minutes. Add the blended cornflour and the mushrooms, and simmer for 1-2 minutes. Serve immediately.

Wonton Soup

PREPARATION TIME: 10 minutes

COOKING TIME: 8 minutes

SERVES: 6 people

20-24 wontons
2 sprigs Chinese parsley, or watercress, finely chopped
1.5 litres (2½ pints) chicken stock
2-3 spring onions, finely chopped
2.5cm (1 inch) fresh root ginger, peeled and finely chopped
Salt to taste
15ml (1 tbsp) soy sauce
Pinch monosodium glutamate (optional)
2.5ml (½ tsp) sugar
Few drops sesame oil
1.25ml (¼ tsp) ground white pepper

Boil wontons in a large saucepan of water for 2-3 minutes until they float to the surface. Remove and drain. Divide cooked wontons and parsley among 6-8 soup bowls. Bring stock to boil and add onions, ginger, salt and the remaining ingredients. Cook for 2-3 minutes, pour over the wontons and serve immediately.

Steamed Shrimp Pancakes

PREPARATION TIME: 1 hour

COOKING TIME: 10-15 minutes

MAKES: 25-30 pancakes

175g (6oz) plain flour or high gluten flour
50g (2oz) cornflour
1.25ml (¼ tsp) salt
15ml (1 tbsp) oil
45ml (3 tbsps) beaten egg
30ml (2 tbsps) water
30ml (2 tbsps) flour mixed with cold water to a smooth paste

Duck Soup (page 10) (top), Chicken and Mushroom Soup (centre right) and Wonton Soup (right).

FILLING
150g (6oz) shrimp, boiled and finely chopped
2 spring onions, bulb only, finely chopped
1.25ml (¼ tsp) salt or to taste
5ml (1 tsp) cornflour to bind

Sieve the flour, cornflour and salt into a bowl. Add the oil, beaten egg and water and mix to make a stiff dough. Leave for 30 minutes to rest. Knead well for 5-6 minutes and roll into 25-30 15-cm (6-inch) circles on greaseproof paper. Place the filling in the centre and flatten. Spread flour-and-water paste around the edge of each pancake and fold up from one end to make a roll. Arrange the pancakes in a greased steamer or Chinese bamboo steamer and cook over boiling water for 10-15 minutes. Serve piping hot with chilli or soy sauce dip.

FILLING
To make the filling, mix together all the ingredients, except the cornflour, and then bind with the cornflour.

ALTERNATIVE
To make rice pancakes, soak 100g (4oz) rice for 10 minutes. Grind with water to make a very fine paste of batter consistency. Add 15ml (1 tbsp) oil and mix well. Line a steamer with fine muslin and spoon in a little batter; spread it out into a thin pancake.

Facing page: Four Happiness Dumplings (page 16) (top left), Steamed Shrimp Pancakes (page 12) (bottom left) and Steamed Open Dumplings (page 12) (right). Facing page: Seafood Hot and Sour Soup (top) and Sweetcorn and Chicken Soup (bottom).

Steam for 5 minutes. Place a little filling on the pancake and roll up. Steam for 10 minutes and serve piping hot with a dip.

Sweetcorn and Chicken Soup

PREPARATION TIME: 15 minutes

COOKING TIME: 45 minutes

SERVES: 4 people

1 chicken, with giblets
225g (8oz) can creamy sweetcorn
1 onion, peeled and chopped roughly
1 carrot, scraped and chopped roughly
1 stick celery, chopped
6 peppercorns
Parsley stalks
1 bay leaf
1 litre (2 pints) water
Salt
Pepper

GARNISH
Chopped parsley or chives

Clean chicken, and cut into quarters. Put into wok with giblets, chopped vegetables, peppercorns, bay leaf, parsley stalks, seasoning and water. Bring to the boil. Reduce heat and simmer for 30 minutes. Strain and return stock to wok. Remove meat from chicken and cut into fine shreds. Add undrained sweetcorn to stock, and bring to boil. Simmer for 5 minutes. Add chicken and cook for 1 minute. Sprinkle with chopped parsley or chives. Serve hot.

Seafood Hot and Sour Soup

PREPARATION TIME: 20 minutes

COOKING TIME: 20 minutes

SERVES: 4 people

2 dried Chinese mushrooms
1 cake fresh beancurd, diced
115g (4oz) prawns or shrimp, shelled and de-veined
600ml (1 pint) light stock, preferably fish stock
60g (2oz) crabmeat, or 2 crab sticks, cut into 1.5cm (½-inch) slices
1 tbsp oyster sauce
15ml (1 tbsp) light soy sauce
15ml (1 tbsp) lemon juice
5ml (½ tsp) lemon rind, cut into slivers
15ml (1 tbsp) vegetable oil
1 red chilli, seeds removed, and finely sliced
2 spring onions, sliced
Salt
Pepper
5ml (1 tsp) sesame oil

GARNISH
Fresh coriander, if desired

Soak mushrooms in hot water and set aside for 20 minutes. Heat wok, add vegetable oil and, when hot, stir-fry prawns, chilli, lemon rind and spring onions. Add stock, oyster sauce and light soy sauce, and bring to the boil. Reduce heat and simmer for 5 minutes. Add salt and pepper to taste. Remove hard stalks from mushrooms and slice caps finely. Add crabmeat, beancurd and Chinese mushrooms to wok, and cook for a further 5 minutes. Stir in lemon juice and sesame oil. Adjust seasoning and serve sprinkled with fresh coriander leaves if desired.

Chilli Prawns

PREPARATION TIME: 10-15 minutes

MICROWAVE COOKING TIME: 4½-5½ minutes

SERVES: 4 people

450g (1lb) king prawns
30ml (2 tbsps) oil
2 cloves garlic, crushed
30ml (2 tbsps) chilli sauce (hot or sweet)
15ml (1 tbsp) rice wine
15ml (1 tbsp) lemon juice
Salt

GARNISH
Chilli pepper flowers

Remove the heads and shells of the prawns, but leave on the very ends of the tails. Wash, de-vein and pat dry. Put the oil and garlic into a bowl and cover with cling film. Cook on HIGH 1 minute. Stir in the chilli sauce, wine, lemon juice and salt. Cook 30 seconds on HIGH. Add the prawns and cook for 3-4 minutes on MEDIUM. Serve hot or cold. Garnish with chilli pepper flowers (see introduction).

Four Happiness Dumplings

PREPARATION TIME: 30-45 minutes for pastry; 20-30 minutes for filling

COOKING TIME: 20 minutes

MAKES: 30-35 dumplings

PASTRY
225g (8oz) plain flour
Pinch of salt
200ml (⅓ pint) boiling water

FILLING
175g (6oz) boned loin of pork, finely chopped or minced
2 black mushrooms, soaked and diced
50g (2oz) mixed vegetables, peeled and finely chopped (peas, carrots, celery, etc.)
2.5ml (½ tsp) brown sugar
10ml (2 tsps) light soy sauce
1.25ml (¼ tsp) freshly ground black pepper
1 egg
5-6 chives, finely chopped
Salt to taste
15ml (1 tbsp) oil
7.5ml (1½ tsps) cornflour
30ml (2 tbsps) flour mixed with a little cold water to a smooth paste

Put the flour and salt into a bowl. Add the boiling water and mix quickly to make a dough. Cover, and allow to stand for 20-30 minutes. Knead the dough for 2-3 minutes, sprinkling the work-surface with a little cornflour if needed. Divide the dough into 30-35 equal portions and roll each one to a circle 6cm (2½ inches) in diameter. Mix the pork with the mushrooms, mixed vegetables, sugar, soy sauce, black pepper, egg, chives and salt to taste. Add the oil and cornflour and mix well with a fork. Divide filling into 30 to 35 equal portions. Fill each dumpling wrapper with a portion of filling and form into crescent-shape dumplings. Steam them in an ordinary steamer or a Chinese bamboo steamer for about 20 minutes. Serve with a dip and chilli sauce. To make the crescent shape, place a wrapper on a flat surface, put a little filling in the centre, spread the edges with a little flour and water paste and pinch the edges of the wrapper together to seal. Pull one corner of the filled wonton around and over the other corner. Press to seal.

Garlic Prawns with Salt and Pepper

PREPARATION TIME: 10-15 minutes

MICROWAVE COOKING TIME: 4½-5½ minutes

SERVES: 4 people

450g (1lb) king prawns
30ml (2 tbsps) oil
2 cloves garlic, minced
45ml (3 tbsps) oyster sauce
30ml (2 tbsps) soy sauce
15ml (1 tbsp) lemon juice
10ml (2 tsps) coarsely ground black pepper
Salt

GARNISH
Spring onion brushes

Prepare the prawns as for Chilli Prawns. Put the oil and garlic into a bowl. Cover and cook 1 minute on HIGH. Add the oyster sauce, soy sauce, lemon juice and cook 30 seconds on HIGH. Stir in the prawns and cook for 3-4 minutes on MEDIUM. Sprinkle with salt and pepper before serving. Garnish with spring onion brushes (see introduction).

Chinese Noodle Soup with Pork Dumplings

PREPARATION TIME: 20 minutes

MICROWAVE COOKING TIME: 10 minutes plus 1 minute standing time

SERVES: 4 people

225g (8oz) minced pork
2.5ml (½ tsp) ground ginger
15ml (1 tbsp) cornflour
30ml (2 tbsps) light soy sauce
1150ml (2 pints) stock
60g (2oz) thin Chinese noodles
15ml (1 tbsp) rice wine
4 spring onions, sliced

Mix the cornflour with the soy sauce. Combine with the pork and ginger. Shape into small balls. Heat the stock 5 minutes on HIGH in a large, deep bowl. Add the pork balls and cook 2 minutes on HIGH. Add the noodles and wine and cook a further 3 minutes on HIGH. Add the spring onions and leave to stand 1 minute before serving.

Facing page: Garlic Prawns with Salt and Pepper (top) and Chilli Prawns (bottom).

Chinese Combination Soup

PREPARATION TIME: 30 minutes

COOKING TIME: 20 minutes

SERVES: 4 people

4 dried Chinese mushrooms
225g (8oz) chicken
115g (4oz) fine/thread egg noodles
1 clove garlic, thinly sliced
5ml (1 tsp) finely sliced root ginger
¼ small cabbage, shredded
600ml (1 pint) chicken stock
15ml (1 tbsp) peanut oil
2 eggs, beaten
15ml (1 tbsp) dark soy sauce
15ml (1 tbsp) sherry
15ml (1 tbsp) water
5ml (1 tsp) cornflour
2 shallots, peeled and sliced finely

Soak mushrooms in hot water for 20 minutes. Remove and discard stems. Slice mushroom caps thinly. Soak noodles in boiling salted water for 2 minutes. Rinse in cold water. Drain. Slice chicken finely. Heat wok and add peanut oil. Add garlic and ginger, and fry gently for 5 minutes, then discard. Add chicken, and fry for a few minutes until meat has turned white. Add mushrooms, shallots, cabbage and stock. Bring to the boil and simmer for 5 minutes. Gradually pour in eggs and stir so that they cook in shreds. Mix cornflour with 15ml (1 tbsp) water, and pour into soup, stirring continously. Cook for 2 minutes or until soup thickens. Add noodles, soy sauce and sherry. Serve immediately.

Sweetcorn and Crabmeat Soup

PREPARATION TIME: 10 minutes

MICROWAVE COOKING TIME:
4 minutes plus 5 minutes standing time

SERVES: 4 people

2 225g (8oz) cans creamed corn
1 onion
1150ml (2 pints) chicken stock
1 small piece ginger root, peeled and grated
5ml (1 tsp) sherry
30ml (2 tbsps) cornflour
225g (8oz) crabmeat
2 spring onions
Salt

Combine the onion and corn in a deep bowl. Cover and cook 1 minute on HIGH to soften onion slightly. Add the ginger, sherry, stock and cornflour mixed with 30ml (2 tbsps) water. Cook for 2-3 minutes until thickened, stirring halfway through cooking. Stir in the crabmeat, reserving about 30ml (2 tbsps) for garnish. Leave to stand, covered, for 3 minutes before serving. Sprinkle reserved crabmeat and spring onion on top of each serving.

This page: Chinese Noodle Soup with Pork Dumplings (page 16) (top) and Sweetcorn and Crabmeat Soup (bottom). Facing page: Chinese Combination Soup (top) and Eggflower Soup (page 20) (bottom).

Eggflower Soup

PREPARATION TIME: 10 minutes

COOKING TIME: 10 minutes

SERVES: 4 people

600ml (1 pint) chicken stock
2 eggs, lightly beaten
15ml (1 tbsp) light soy sauce
400g (14oz) can plum tomatoes
2 spring onions, chopped finely

Drain and chop tomatoes, removing seeds, and reserve juice. Bring soy sauce, tomato juice and stock to the boil in the wok. Add tomatoes and half the spring onions, and cook for 2 minutes. Dribble beaten egg in gradually, stirring continuously. Serve immediately, sprinkled with remaining spring onions.

Steamed Crabmeat and Egg Custard

PREPARATION TIME: 30 minutes

MICROWAVE COOKING TIME: 8-9 minutes

SERVES: 4 people

2 eggs, beaten
140ml (¼ pint) chicken stock
15ml (1 tbsp) sherry
180g (6oz) cooked crabmeat
4 chopped spring onions
3 chopped water chestnuts
2 finely chopped Chinese mushrooms, pre-cooked 30 minutes
15ml (1 tsp) grated fresh ginger root
Salt

Mix together the eggs, stock, and sherry, and add the remaining ingredients. Spoon into lightly oiled ramekins. Cover loosely and arrange in a circle on the turntable and cook 1 minute on HIGH. Reduce to LOW/DEFROST and cook for 7-8 minutes or until softly set. Unmould onto plates and serve with soy sauce. Surround with shredded Chinese leaves if desired.

Wonton Wrappers

PREPARATION TIME: 5-6 hours (including standing time)

MAKES: 40-50 wrappers

120g (4¼oz) high gluten flour
30ml (2 tbsps) beaten egg
30ml (2 tbsps) cold water
Cornflour

Sieve flour and gradually add the beaten egg and water mixed together. Mix to a stiff dough. Knead firmly for 5-6 minutes and wrap in cling film. Leave to stand at room temperature for 4-5 hours. Roll out into a very large square on a work-surface dusted with cornflour. The pastry should be almost transparent. Cut into 40-50 7.5cm (3-inch) round or square wrappers. Dust each wrapper with cornflour before stacking. Store the wrappers, wrapped securely in cling film, in the refrigerator for up to 24 hours. If they are allowed to dry out they will split during cooking.

Spring Roll Wrappers

PREPARATION TIME: 20 minutes, plus chilling time

MAKES: 12 wrappers

100g (4oz) strong plain flour
1 egg, beaten
A little cold water

Sieve the flour into a bowl. Make a well in the centre and add the beaten egg and a little cold water. Mix to a soft yet firm dough, adding a little extra water if necessary. Knead the dough until it is really pliable. Chill, covered, for 4 hours or overnight. Allow to come back to room temperature. Roll out the dough on a well-floured surface to about 5mm (¼ inch) thick. Cut into 12 equal pieces, and then roll each piece to a square about 15x15cm (6x6 inches) – each square should be very thin.

Right: Steamed Crabmeat and Egg Custard.

Wontons with Pork and Shrimp Filling

PREPARATION TIME: 30 minutes

COOKING TIME: 10-15 minutes

MAKES: 40-50 wontons

175g (6oz) lean pork, minced
Oil
175g (6oz) peeled shrimp, finely chopped
3 spring onions, finely chopped
2.5ml (½ tsp) ground white pepper
15ml (1 tbsp) soy sauce
7.5ml (1½ tsp) rice wine or dry sherry
2.5ml (½ tsp) salt, or to taste
7.5ml (1½ tsp) cornflour blended with 30ml (2 tbsps) water
40-50 wonton wrappers
30ml (2 tbsps) plain flour, mixed to a smooth paste with a little cold water

Fry pork in 30ml (2 tbsps) oil until it loses its pink colour. Add shrimp and onions and fry for 3-4 minutes. Add pepper, soy sauce and wine. Season with salt and stir-fry for 1-2 minutes. Add the blended cornflour and stir over a moderate heat until thickened. Allow to cool before filling the wontons. Divide filling into 40-50 equal portions. Take a wonton wrapper, moisten the edges with the flour-and-water paste. Place a portion of filling in the centre of the wonton and gather up the edges to make a neat round, or shape in such a way as to make a triangle or any other shape that you prefer. Once you have shaped all the wontons, deep-fry them in hot oil until crisp and golden. You will need to fry them in 3 or more batches. Drain well on absorbent paper before serving.

Spring Rolls

PREPARATION TIME: 20-30 minutes

COOKING TIME: about 20 minutes

MAKES: 12 rolls

225g (8oz) lean, raw pork or beef, finely shredded
100g (4oz) prawns or shrimp (either uncooked or boiled), shelled
4 spring onions, finely chopped
Cooking oil
10ml (2 tsps) fresh root ginger, peeled and shredded
100g (4oz) white cabbage, shredded
75g (3oz) bean sprouts
15ml (1 tbsp) soy sauce
Salt to taste
12 spring roll wrappers, each 15cm (6 inches) square (see recipe)
30ml (2 tbsps) plain flour, mixed to a smooth paste with a little cold water

Fry the shredded pork, prawns or shrimp and the spring onions in 15ml (1 tbsp) cooking oil for 2-3 minutes. Add the ginger, cabbage and bean sprouts, and stir-fry for 2-3 minutes.

Facing page: Fried Meat Dumplings (top right), Spring Rolls (centre left) and Wontons with Pork and Shrimp Filling (bottom). Above: Crab Rolls (page 24) (top) and Rice Paper Prawn Parcels (page 24) (bottom). Above right: Egg Drop Soup (page 24) (top), Crab and Watercress Soup (page 26) (centre) and Crab and Sweetcorn Soup (page 28) (bottom).

Add soy sauce, and season with a little salt if desired. Remove from the heat and allow to cool. Lay out the spring roll wrappers on a clean work surface, with one point of each wrapper facing you. Divide the filling mixture into 12 equal portions and place one portion of filling just above the front point of each wrapper. Fold in the opposite side points, so that they overlap slightly like an envelope – secure the side points with a little flour and water paste. Starting with the point facing you, roll each wrapper up around the filling, securing the remaining point with a little flour and water paste. Repeat in exactly the same way with the remaining spring roll wrappers. The rolls will keep a better shape if you chill them for 1 hour before cooking. Deep-fry over a medium heat until golden brown and crisp. Drain thoroughly on absorbent paper and serve hot with a selection of dips or chilli sauce. The spring rolls can be frozen, uncooked.

Fried Meat Dumplings

PREPARATION TIME: 10 minutes

COOKING TIME: about 15 minutes

MAKES: 48 dumplings

30ml (2 tbsps) cooking oil
225g (8oz) lean minced beef or lamb
2 spring onions, chopped
30ml (2 tbsps) light soy sauce
2.5ml (½ tsp) salt
22.5ml (1½ tbsps) rice wine or dry sherry
10ml (2 tsps) cornflour mixed with 30ml (2 tbsps) water
Dumpling wrappers (see recipe)
30ml (2 tbsps) plain flour mixed to a paste with cold water
Oil for deep frying

Heat the 30ml (2 tbsps) oil in a pan and fry the minced meat and onion for 2-3 minutes. Add the soy sauce, salt and wine. Cook gently for 2 minutes and then stir in the cornflour and water mixture. Stir over the heat until the mixture thickens. Put the meat mixture into a dish and leave to cool. Divide into equal portions – about 48. Take a round dumpling wrapper and place a portion of filling in the centre. Moisten the edges of the wrapper with a little flour and water paste, gather the edges up and over the filling and pinch together to seal. Shape neatly. Continue to make the remaining dumplings in the same way. Deep-fry the dumplings in moderately hot oil, cooking a few dumplings at a time, until they are golden brown. Drain thoroughly on absorbent paper. Serve with chilli sauce dip.

Steamed Barbecued Pork Dumplings

PREPARATION TIME: 20 minutes

MICROWAVE COOKING TIME: 17-18 minutes per batch

SERVES: 4 people

10ml (2 tsps) oil
300g (10oz) minced pork
1 clove garlic, minced
Pinch sugar
30ml (2 tbsps) soy sauce
30ml (2 tbsps) cornflour mixed with 45ml (3 tbsps) stock
120ml (4 fl oz) hoisin sauce
30 wonton wrappers

Combine oil, pork and garlic in a casserole dish. Cover and cook on HIGH 5 minutes, breaking up the pork frequently with a fork as it cooks. Mix together the sugar, soy sauce, cornflour and stock. Add to the pork and cook a further 2-3 minutes until sauce thickens and clears. Stir in the hoisin sauce. Fill the wonton wrappers and pinch the edges together, but leave some of the filling exposed. Place in one layer in a shallow dish, and barely cover with water. Cover the dish with cling film and cook 2 minutes on HIGH and 8 minutes on LOW/DEFROST. Serve hot.

Egg Drop Soup

PREPARATION TIME: 10 minutes

COOKING TIME: 8 minutes

SERVES: 6 people

This soup derives its name from stirring beaten eggs into the boiling hot soup. On hitting the soup, the egg cooks and forms threads. The eggs can also be carefully dropped in whole, so that they cook without breaking.

1.5 litres (2½ pints) chicken stock
3 spring onions, finely chopped
75g (3oz) frozen peas, or shelled fresh peas
1 bunch watercress, finely chopped
A few thin slices of fresh root ginger
Salt and freshly ground black pepper to taste
15ml (1 tbsp) light soy sauce
Pinch monosodium glutamate (optional)
5ml (1 tsp) cornflour blended with 15ml (1 tbsp) water
4 eggs, beaten (or 6-8 whole eggs, see below)

Bring the chicken stock to the boil with the spring onions, peas, watercress, ginger and salt and pepper to taste. Allow to simmer for 2-3 minutes. Add the soy sauce, monosodium glutamate and the blended cornflour. Stir well until the soup is transparent and thick. Bring the soup back to the boil and stir in the beaten eggs. Serve immediately. Alternatively, put a whole egg into each warm soup bowl and ladle the hot soup over the top.

Crab Rolls

PREPARATION TIME: 20 minutes

COOKING TIME: 20 minutes

MAKES: 12 rolls

175g (6oz) crabmeat, fresh or canned
3 spring onions, finely sliced
12 spring roll wrappers
30g (1oz) cellophane noodles
1.25ml (¼ tsp) grated root ginger
5ml (1 tsp) oyster sauce
30ml (2 tbsps) finely chopped bamboo shoots
Salt
Vegetable or peanut oil for deep frying

Soak cellophane noodles in hot water for 8 minutes, or as directed, and drain. Flake crabmeat, and drain if necessary. Combine crabmeat with spring onions, noodles, ginger, bamboo shoots, oyster sauce, and salt to taste. Place spring roll wrappers with one corner pointing towards you. Spoon some of the mixture just before the centre. Fold over the corner nearest you and roll to centre. Fold the two side points into the centre, and roll up completely. They may be sealed with a paste of flour and water if necessary. Refrigerate until needed. Heat oil in wok and deep-fry batches of crab rolls just before serving. Drain on absorbent paper. Serve warm with ginger sauce or sweet-and-sour sauce.

Rice Paper Prawn Parcels

PREPARATION TIME: 15 minutes

COOKING TIME: 15 minutes

MAKES: about 20 parcels

225g (8oz) prawns shelled and de-veined
6 spring onions, sliced finely
1 packet rice paper
White of 1 egg
2.5ml (½ tsp) cornflour
150ml (¼ pint) peanut oil
5ml (1 tsp) Chinese wine, or 10ml (2 tsps) dry sherry
5ml (1 tsp) light soy sauce
5ml (1 tsp) sugar
Salt
Pepper

Dry prepared prawns on absorbent paper. Mix egg white, cornflour, wine, sugar, soy sauce, spring onions and seasoning together. Mix in prawns. Heat peanut oil in wok until hot. Wrap five or six prawns in each piece of rice paper. Gently drop in rice paper parcels and deep-fry for about 5 minutes. Serve hot.

Steamed Chicken Wontons

PREPARATION TIME: 20 minutes

MICROWAVE COOKING TIME: 10 minutes per batch

SERVES: 4 people

300g (10oz) minced chicken
2 chopped spring onions
2 chopped water chestnuts
Small piece ginger root, peeled and grated
30ml (2 tbsps) light soy sauce
15ml (1 tbsp) rice wine
15ml (1 tbsp) sesame oil
1 egg, beaten
Pinch sugar
Salt and pepper
30 fresh wonton wrappers

Mince raw chicken in a food processor and combine with the remaining ingredients except the wonton

Facing page: Steamed Chicken Wontons (top) and Steamed Barbecued Pork Dumplings (bottom) – served with Sweet and Sour and Hot Mustard Sauces.

wrappers. Place a teaspoonful of the mixture in the centre of each wonton and twist the ends together to seal. Brush lightly with water if the ends won't stick together. Place wontons in one layer in a casserole dish and barely cover with water. Cover with cling film. Cook in 2 batches for 2 minutes on HIGH and 8 minutes on LOW/DEFROST. Remove with a draining spoon. Serve with Sweet and Sour and Hot Mustard sauces.

Hot and Sour Soup

PREPARATION TIME: 30 minutes

COOKING TIME: 30 minutes

SERVES: 4 people

115g (4oz) lean pork fillet
4 dried Chinese mushrooms
60g (2oz) bamboo shoots, sliced
1 square beancurd, diced
30ml (2 tbsps) sunflower or vegetable oil
1 litre (2 pints) light, clear stock, or hot water plus 2 chicken stock cubes
5ml (1 tsp) cornflour
30ml (2 tbsps) cold water
5ml (1 tsp) sesame oil

MARINADE
15ml (1 tbsp) light soy sauce
45ml (3 tbsps) brown vinegar
30ml (2 tbsps) water
5ml (1 tsp) sesame oil
Salt
Pepper

GARNISH
Fresh coriander

Soak Chinese mushrooms for 20 minutes in hot water. Meanwhile, slice pork into thin slivers. Make the marinade by combining light soy sauce, brown vinegar, water, sesame oil, and salt and pepper. Pour over pork and leave for 30 minutes. Drain mushrooms. Remove and discard stalks. Slice caps very finely. Remove pork from marinade, and reserve marinade. Heat wok, and add sunflower or vegetable oil. When hot, stir-fry pork, mushrooms and bamboo shoots for 2 minutes. Add stock and bring to the boil. Simmer for 10 minutes. Add beancurd, marinade, and salt and pepper to taste. Slake cornflour in 30ml (2 tbsps) of cold water. Add to soup and allow to simmer for 5 minutes. Add sesame oil and sprinkle with fresh coriander. Serve hot.

Chicken and Asparagus Soup

PREPARATION TIME: 10 minutes

COOKING TIME: 45 minutes

SERVES: 4 people

450g (1lb) chicken pieces
1 onion, peeled and roughly chopped
1 carrot, roughly chopped
1 stick celery, roughly chopped
4 peppercorns
300g (10oz) can asparagus pieces
1 litre (2 pints) water
Salt
Pepper

GARNISH
Chopped parsley

Remove chicken meat from bones and cut into fine shreds. Put chicken bones, onion, carrot, celery, peppercorns and water in wok, and season with salt and pepper. Bring to the boil, reduce heat, and simmer for 30 minutes. Strain and return stock to wok. Add chicken shreds, and simmer until chicken is cooked. Add undrained asparagus pieces. Adjust seasoning. Serve sprinkled with chopped parsley.

Crab and Watercress Soup

PREPARATION TIME: 10 minutes

COOKING TIME: 8-9 minutes

SERVES: 6 people

1.5 litres (2½ pints) chicken stock
100g (4oz) white crabmeat, shredded
2 spring onions, finely chopped
2 bunches watercress, finely chopped
Salt and freshly ground black pepper to taste
5ml (1 tsp) cornflour or arrowroot
15ml (1 tbsp) water
10ml (2 tsp) light soy sauce
A few drops sesame oil

Chicken and Asparagus Soup (below) and Hot and Sour Soup (right).

Bring the stock to the boil with the crabmeat, onions and watercress, and simmer for 4-5 minutes. Add salt and pepper to taste. Mix the cornflour with the water and add to the soup. Allow to simmer for a further 2 minutes. Add soy sauce and sesame oil, mix well and simmer for 2 minutes. Serve immediately.

Spring Rolls

PREPARATION TIME: 20 minutes

COOKING TIME: 30 minutes

MAKES: 12 rolls

225g (8oz) finely minced pork
1 red chilli, seeds removed, and sliced finely
10 canned water chestnuts, chopped
1 onion, peeled and finely chopped
1 clove garlic, crushed
2.5ml (½ tsp) grated root ginger
5ml (1 tsp) ground turmeric
30ml (2 tbsps) peanut oil
12 spring roll wrappers
Salt
Pepper
Peanut or vegetable oil for deep frying

Heat wok, add 30ml (2 tbsps) peanut oil, and fry garlic, ginger, ground turmeric and onion for 3 minutes. Add pork, and stir-fry until meat is browning. Add water chestnuts, chilli, and salt and pepper to taste, and fry for a further 2 minutes. Remove from wok and set aside to cool. Place spring roll wrapper with one corner pointing towards you. Spoon some of the mixture just in front of the centre. Fold over the corner nearest to you, and roll to centre. Fold the two side points into the centre and finish rolling up. The rolls may be sealed with a paste of flour and water if necessary. Refrigerate until needed. Heat oil for deep frying in wok, and deep-fry spring rolls in batches just before needed. Drain on absorbent paper, and serve warm with chilli or sweet-and-sour sauce.

Prawn and Lettuce Soup

PREPARATION TIME: 10 minutes

MICROWAVE COOKING TIME: 12 minutes plus 5 minutes standing time

SERVES: 4 people

360g (12oz) peeled prawns
120g (4oz) rice
1150ml (2 pints) hot chicken stock
1 piece fresh ginger root, grated
1 small head lettuce, shredded
Salt

Put the rice, stock and ginger into a large, deep bowl. Partially cover and cook 12 minutes on HIGH, stirring often. Cook until the rice softens completely. Add the prawns, lettuce and salt. Leave the soup to stand, covered, for 5 minutes. Prawns should heat through in the stock.

Prawn Toast

PREPARATION TIME: 15 minutes

COOKING TIME: 15 minutes

MAKES: approximately 20 pieces

225g (8oz) prawns, shelled, de-veined and finely chopped
1 small egg, beaten
10ml (2 tsps) sherry
10ml (2 tsps) oyster sauce
2.5ml (½ tsp) grated root ginger
10ml (2 tsps) cornflour
Salt
5 slices white bread
Oil for deep frying

Combine prawns, beaten egg, sherry, oyster sauce, grated ginger, cornflour and a pinch of salt. Using a 4cm (1½-inch) round pastry cutter, cut out circles of bread. Spread mixture on each piece of bread to cover well. Heat oil in wok for deep frying. Fry in batches with bread side up first, until bread is golden brown. Remove and drain on absorbent paper. Keep hot until all frying is completed.

Crab and Sweetcorn Soup

PREPARATION TIME: 8 minutes

COOKING TIME: 8 minutes

SERVES: 6 people

45ml (3 tbsps) water or stock
30ml (2 tbsps) cornflour or arrowroot
1.5 litres (2½ pints) chicken stock
275-350g (10-12oz) creamed sweetcorn
100-175g (4-6oz) crabmeat, shredded
Salt and freshly ground black pepper to taste
5ml (1 tsp) soy sauce
Pinch monosodium glutamate (optional)

Blend cornflour and water together. Bring the stock to the boil in a large pan. Add the sweetcorn, crab, salt and pepper to taste, soy sauce and monosodium glutamate. Simmer for 4-5 minutes. Add the blended cornflour to the soup and stir over a gentle heat until the soup thickens. Serve immediately. Whisked egg whites can be stirred into the hot soup just before serving, if liked.

Facing page: Prawn Toast (top) and Spring Rolls (bottom).

Chinese COOKING

RICE, NOODLES AND EGGS

Rice Noodles Singapore Style

PREPARATION TIME: 15 minutes, plus soaking time for noodles

COOKING TIME: about 15 minutes

SERVES: 4-6 people

225g (8oz) rice noodles
Oil
2 eggs, beaten
1.25cm (½ inch) fresh root ginger, peeled and shredded
100g (4oz) bean sprouts
100g (4oz) cooked ham, pork or chicken, shredded
50g (2oz) chives, finely chopped
2 cloves garlic, finely chopped
Salt to taste
15ml (1 tbsp) chicken stock
30ml (2 tbsps) soy sauce
3 spring onions, chopped

Soak the rice noodles in warm water for 10 minutes and then drain well. Heat 15ml (1 tbsp) oil in a frying pan or wok and fry the beaten eggs to make a thin pancake. Slide onto a plate and cut into thin strips. Heat the wok or frying pan and add 15ml (1 tbsp) oil. Fry the ginger and bean sprouts for 2 minutes. Slide onto a plate. Heat the wok or frying pan with a further 15ml (1 tbsp) oil and fry the pork or chicken and the chives for 1-2 minutes. Slide onto a plate. Heat 30ml (2 tbsps) oil in the wok or frying pan and brown the garlic. Add the rice noodles and stir-fry for 2-3 minutes. Add salt to taste, chicken stock, bean sprouts and pork or chicken. Mix well, sprinkle with soy sauce and stir over the heat for 1 minute. Top with the strips of egg pancake and spring onions and serve immediately.

Noodles in Soup

PREPARATION TIME: 10 minutes

COOKING TIME: 6-8 minutes

SERVES: 4-6 people

450g (1lb) small rounds of noodle cakes
Salt
1.3 litres (2¼ pints) chicken stock
100g (4oz) cooked shredded chicken
2 eggs, hard boiled and sliced
100g (4oz) Chinese napa cabbage, finely shredded (or iceberg lettuce)
2 spring onions, thinly sliced

Cook the noodles in boiling, salted water for 5 minutes. Drain thoroughly. Heat the stock and add salt to taste. Serve the cooked noodles in bowls, and pour over the hot stock. Garnish with chicken, sliced eggs, cabbage and spring onions.

Meat and Prawn Chow Mein

PREPARATION TIME: 20 minutes

COOKING TIME: 12-15 minutes

SERVES: 4-6 people

450g (1lb) dried Chinese noodles or broken spaghetti
Salt to taste
60ml (4 tbsps) oil
2-3 spring onions, chopped
100g (4oz) cooked ham, shredded
100g (4oz) peeled prawns
100g (4oz) shredded carrots
100g (4oz) green beans, sliced
5ml (1 tsp) sugar
15ml (1 tbsp) rice wine or dry sherry
100g (4oz) cooked chicken, shredded
100g (4oz) bean sprouts
37ml (2½ tbsps) soy sauce

Cook the noodles in boiling, salted water for 4-5 minutes. Rinse under cold water and drain thoroughly. Toss in 15ml (1 tbsp) oil. Heat the remaining oil in a wok. Add the onions, ham, prawns, carrots and green beans and stir-fry for 2-3 minutes. Add the salt, sugar, wine, chicken and bean sprouts. Cook for 2 minutes. Add the cooked noodles and soy sauce. Cook for 1-2 minutes. Serve immediately.

Egg Pancakes with Filling

PREPARATION TIME: 10 minutes

COOKING TIME: 6-7 minutes for each pancake

SERVES: 4-6 people

6 eggs
Salt and freshly ground black pepper to taste

Facing page: Meat and Prawn Chow Mein (top), Noodles in Soup (centre) and Rice Noodles Singapore Style (bottom).

P
S

This page: Eight Precious Rice (page 42) (top) and Ham and Bean Fried Rice (bottom). Facing page: Prawns in Egg Custard (page 34) (top left), Egg Pancakes with Filling (page 30) (top right), Shrimp Fu Yung (page 36) (centre left) and Egg Fu Yung (bottom right).

100g (4oz) lean pork, finely chopped or ground
50g (2oz) button mushrooms, chopped
5ml (1 tsp) rice wine or dry sherry
5ml (1 tsp) light soy sauce
2.5ml (½ tsp) sugar
2.5ml (½ tsp) fresh root ginger, minced
Oil

Beat the eggs and season with salt and pepper. Mix the pork with the mushrooms, wine, soy sauce, sugar and ginger. Add salt and pepper to taste and mix well. Heat the wok and add 5ml (1 tsp) oil. Spoon in 30ml (2 tbsps) of the beaten egg and spread into a 7.5cm (3-inch) circle. Place 10ml (2 tsps) filling into the centre of the egg. When the underside of the egg sets but the top is still moist, fold the egg circle over to make a crescent shape; press gently to seal the edges. Cook for 4 minutes on a low heat to cook the filling. Make the remaining pancakes in the same way. Serve with a chilli sauce.

Ham and Bean Fried Rice

PREPARATION TIME: 15 minutes

MICROWAVE COOKING TIME: 9 minutes plus 2 minutes standing time

SERVES: 4 people

45ml (3 tbsps) oil
2 eggs, beaten
Salt and pepper
120g (4oz) ham, chopped
120g (4oz) French beans, cut in thin, diagonal slices
225g (8oz) cooked rice
15ml (1 tbsp) soy sauce
4 spring onions, chopped

Heat a browning dish 5 minutes on HIGH. Pour in half the oil and half the beaten egg and cook for 30 seconds on HIGH on one side. Turn over and cook for 30 seconds on the other side. Repeat with remaining egg. Keep the egg warm and add the remaining oil to the dish. Heat for 1 minute on HIGH and add the ham. Cover the dish and cook for 1 minute on HIGH. Add the rice and cook, covered, for 5 minutes on HIGH. Add the beans, soy sauce and onions. Cook 1 minute on HIGH and toss the ingredients to mix well. Slice the eggs into thin strips and scatter over the top of the rice. Cover the dish and leave to stand for 2 minutes before serving.

Egg Fu Yung

PREPARATION TIME: 5 minutes

COOKING TIME: 8-10 minutes

SERVES: 3-4 people

6 eggs
22.5ml (1½ tbsps) soy sauce
3-4 spring onions, chopped
Salt and freshly ground black pepper to taste
45ml (3 tbsps) oil
100g (4oz) bean sprouts

Beat the eggs and soy sauce together and add the spring onions and salt and pepper to taste. Heat the oil in a frying pan or wok and stir-fry the bean sprouts for 2-3 minutes. Pour in the beaten egg

mixture. Leave over a moderate heat to set and then put under the grill to set and brown the top. Cut into wedges and serve immediately. Alternatively, stir the mixture while it is cooking so that it turns out like scrambled egg.

Prawns in Egg Custard

PREPARATION TIME: 5 minutes

COOKING TIME: 20 minutes

SERVES: 6 people

8 eggs
Salt and freshly ground black pepper to taste
Pinch monosodium glutamate
5ml (1 tsp) Shao Hsing wine
300ml (½ pint) chicken stock
300ml (½ pint) water
450g (1lb) prawns, peeled
10ml (2 tsps) cooked oil

Beat the eggs in a bowl, add the seasoning, monosodium glutamate and wine. Bring the stock and water to the boil and add to the eggs. Add prawns and set the bowl over a steamer. Cover and steam over simmering water for about 15-20 minutes, until the custard has set. Serve with the cooked oil spooned over the top.

Plain Rice

PREPARATION TIME: 5 minutes

COOKING TIME: 5-7 minutes

SERVES: 4-6 people

450g (1lb) rice
Pinch salt
10ml (2 tsps) oil

To make a bowl of plain rice, take any grade of long or medium-grained rice. Wash the rice in 4-5 changes of water and then add enough cold water to come 2.5cm (1 inch) above the rice level. Add the salt and oil and bring to the boil. Stir once. Cover and simmer gently for 5-7 minutes, until the water has been totally absorbed. Remove from the heat and serve. Plain boiled rice should be fluffy, yet have enough moisture around the rice so that the grains can be easily picked up with chopsticks.

Sizzling Rice or Singing Rice

PREPARATION TIME: 50 minutes

COOKING TIME: *2 hours, plus time for deep frying sizzling rice*

100g (4oz) short-grained rice

When rice is cooked, the crust that forms on the bottom of the pot can be dried and then deep fried. When it is immersed in gravy or soup it makes a sizzling noise, hence the name. Once made or collected, the rice crusts can be kept for months.

TO MAKE A RICE CRUST
Wash rice in 4-5 changes of water, until the water runs clear. Drain the rice and put it into a pan with 300ml (½ pint) of water; bring to the boil. Reduce heat to low and cook for 20 minutes,

Shrimp Egg Rice (page 36) (below), Sizzling Rice or Singing Rice (bottom left) and Plain Rice (bottom right).

simmering gently. Turn off the heat and let the rice stand, covered, for 25-30 minutes. Take a non-stick frying pan and transfer the rice to it. Spread evenly to a thickness of 1cm (½ inch). Cook on very gentle heat for 40-50 minutes. Turn over and cook gently for another hour. The rice should be very dry. Break into 5cm (2-inch) squares and store in a glass jar with a lid.

TO COOK SIZZLING RICE
Pour oil into a pan to a depth of 5cm (2 inches) and bring to a moderately high temperature (190°C or 375°F). Add the rice squares and fry until golden brown. Remove and drain on kitchen paper. Serve with soup or any stir-fried dish.

Tossed Noodles

PREPARATION TIME: 20 minutes

MICROWAVE COOKING TIME: 10 minutes plus 5 minutes standing time

SERVES: 6 people

450g (1lb) Chinese egg noodles
1150ml (2 pints) boiling water
120ml (4oz) soy sauce mixed with 30ml (2 tbsps) cornflour
90g (3oz) lean steak, cut in short, thin strips
15ml (1 tbsp) oil
120ml (4 fl oz) brown stock
4 spring onions, sliced
½ cucumber, sliced
1 small piece white radish, diced
Fresh coriander leaves

Cook noodles as for Velvet Noodles. Heat a browning dish 5 minutes on HIGH. Pour in the oil and add the steak. Cook 2 minutes on HIGH. Stir in the soy sauce, cornflour and the stock. Cover and cook 3 minutes on HIGH. Add more stock if the sauce is too thick. Add the onions, cucumber and radish to the sauce, and leave to stand 5 minutes before serving. Pour over noodles and toss before serving. Garnish with whole coriander leaves.

Shrimp Egg Rice

PREPARATION TIME: 20 minutes

COOKING TIME: 17-18 minutes

SERVES: 4-6 people

450g (1lb) long- or medium-grained rice
2 eggs
2.5ml (½ tsp) salt
60ml (4 tbsps) oil
2 spring onions, chopped
1 large onion, peeled and chopped
2 cloves garlic, peeled and chopped
100g (4oz) peeled shrimp
50g (2oz) shelled peas
30ml (2 tbsps) dark soy sauce

TO COOK THE RICE
Wash rice in 4-5 changes of water. Add cold water to 2.5cm (1 inch) above the rice level and bring to the boil. Stir once and reduce the heat to simmer. Cover the pan and gently cook for 5-7 minutes, until the rice is dry and the liquid has been totally absorbed. Remove from the heat, add cold water to cover and drain thoroughly. Spread the rice on a serving tray and separate the grains with a fork.
Beat the eggs in a bowl and season with a pinch of salt. Heat the wok and add 15ml (1 tbsp) oil. Add the onions and stir-fry for 2 minutes. Add the beaten eggs. Allow to set slightly and then stir the mixture until it scrambles. Remove onto a plate. Heat the wok and add 15ml (1 tbsp) oil. Fry the garlic for 1 minute then add the shrimp and cook for 2 minutes. Add the peas, and stir-fry for 1 minute. Remove onto a plate. Heat the wok and add the remaining oil, a little salt to taste, and the cooked rice. Stir-fry to heat the rice through. Stir in the soy sauce, shrimp mixture and the cooked eggs, gently stirring the mixture to blend. Serve immediately.

Shrimp Fu Yung

PREPARATION TIME: 10 minutes

COOKING TIME: 4 minutes for filling; 3-4 minutes for each pancake

SERVES: 6 people

Oil
1-2 cloves of garlic, chopped
100g (4oz) shrimp, peeled
100g (4oz) green beans, sliced
1 carrot, shredded
6 eggs
Salt and freshly ground black pepper to taste
250ml (8 fl oz) chicken stock
1.25ml (¼ tsp) salt
10ml (2 tsps) soy sauce
5ml (1 tsp) sugar
5ml (1 tsp) vinegar
5ml (1 tsp) cornflour

Heat 30ml (2 tbsps) oil in a wok. Add the garlic and stir-fry for 1 minute. Add the shrimp and stir-fry for 1 minute. Add the beans and carrots and stir-fry for 2 minutes. Remove and keep on one side. Beat the eggs with salt and pepper to taste, and add the cooled shrimp mixture. Clean the wok and heat 5ml (1 tsp) oil. Pour in 60ml (4 tbsps) of the egg mixture and cook like a pancake. When the egg is set, turn the pancake over and cook on the other side until lightly golden. Place on a warm platter and keep warm.

TO MAKE THE SAUCE
Beat the stock with the other sauce ingredients and stir over a gentle heat until the sauce thickens. Serve the pancakes with this sauce.

Velvet Noodles

PREPARATION TIME: 20 minutes

MICROWAVE COOKING TIME: 8-12 minutes plus 5 minutes standing time

SERVES: 6 people

25ml (1½ tbsps) light soy sauce
15ml (1 tbsp) cornflour
Dash sesame oil
90g (3oz) lean pork cut in small, thin slices
60g (2oz) mushrooms, sliced
570ml (1 pint) chicken stock
Salt
1150ml (2 pints) boiling water
450g (1lb) medium Chinese noodles
½ head Chinese leaves, shredded

Mix soy sauce, cornflour and sesame oil together in a large bowl. Stir in the stock gradually and add the pork and mushrooms. Cover and cook for 5-8 minutes on HIGH, or until pork is cooked. Add the Chinese leaves and leave to stand, covered, while cooking the noodles. Put the noodles and water into a large, deep bowl. Cook for 3 minutes on HIGH, stirring occasionally. Leave to stand 5 minutes before serving. Add salt to the mushrooms and pork if desired. Drain the noodles and arrange on a serving dish. Pour over the sauce and toss before serving.

Facing page: Tossed Noodles (top) and Velvet Noodles (bottom).

Subgum Fried Rice

PREPARATION TIME: 15 minutes

MICROWAVE COOKING TIME:
7 minutes plus 2 minutes standing time

SERVES: 4 people

45ml (3 tbsps) oil
225g (8oz) cooked rice
2 sticks celery, cut into small dice
60g (2oz) mushrooms, roughly chopped
½ red pepper, diced
3 eggs, beaten
15ml (1 tbsp) light soy sauce
Dash sesame oil
Salt and pepper

GARNISH
2 spring onions, sliced diagonally

Heat oil in a large bowl for 1 minute on HIGH. Add the rice and cook 5 minutes on HIGH, covered. Stir in the eggs, soy sauce and vegetables, and cook 2 minutes on HIGH. Add the sesame oil, salt and pepper, and leave to stand 2 minutes before serving. Garnish with onions.

Fried Rice with Egg

PREPARATION TIME: 15 minutes

MICROWAVE COOKING TIME:
8-10 minutes plus standing time

SERVES: 4 people

45ml (3 tbsps) oil
2 spring onions, finely chopped
225g (8oz) cooked rice
3 eggs, beaten
10ml (2 tsps) white wine
Salt and pepper
Dash sesame oil

GARNISH
2 spring onions, shredded

Put the oil and the finely chopped onions into a large bowl and heat for 1 minute on HIGH. Add the rice and cook for 5-7 minutes on HIGH, until very hot. Stir in the eggs, wine, salt, pepper and sesame oil, and cook for 2

Fried Rice with Egg (top) and Subgum Fried Rice (bottom).

minutes on HIGH. Stir carefully and leave to stand, covered, several minutes before serving. Garnish with the shredded onions. Serve with soy sauce, or as an accompaniment to other dishes.

Stir-Fried Eggs with Shredded Meats and Vegetables

PREPARATION TIME: 15-20 minutes

COOKING TIME: 15 minutes

SERVES: 4 people

50g (2oz) cooked chicken, shredded
75g (3oz) cooked pork or beef, shredded
Salt to taste
1.25ml (¼ tsp) soy sauce
60ml (4 tbsps) oil
4 eggs, beaten
2 spring onions, chopped
50g (2oz) dried mushrooms, soaked and sliced
50g (2oz) button mushrooms, sliced
2 cloud ear fungus, boiled in water for 3 minutes and thinly sliced
175g (6oz) Chinese white cabbage, broccoli or green leafy cabbage, shredded
1-2 green or red chillis, chopped
2 sprigs coriander, chopped
Pinch monosodium glutamate (optional)

Put the chicken and pork into a bowl with 1.25ml (¼ tsp) salt and the soy sauce. Leave for 10 minutes. Heat the wok and add 30ml (2 tbsps) oil. Add the beaten eggs and stir-fry for 2-3 minutes until they resemble scrambled egg. Keep on one side. Reheat the wok and add the remaining oil. Fry the onions and meats for 2 minutes. Remove from the wok and keep on one side. Stir-fry the cabbage and chillies in the wok for 1-2 minutes. Cover and gently cook in its own juice until tender – approx 3-4 minutes. Return the meats, mushrooms and egg to the cabbage and add the coriander and monosodium glutamate. Stir-fry for 1-2 minutes. Serve with extra soy sauce and Shao Hsing wine sprinkled over it, if desired.

Above left: Vegetable Rice (top), Assorted Meat Congee (page 42) (centre right) and Rice Supreme (page 42) (bottom). Above: Noodles with Beef and Almonds (page 43) (top), Egg Noodles with Meat Sauce (page 44) (centre) and Fried Noodles with Shredded Chicken (bottom). Facing page: Marbled Eggs (page 42) (top), Noodles with Pork Fu Yung (centre right) and Stir-Fried Eggs with Shredded Meat and Vegetables (bottom left).

Noodles with Pork Fu Yung

PREPARATION TIME: 20 minutes

COOKING TIME: about 20 minutes

SERVES: 4 people

2.5ml (½ tsp) bicarbonate of soda
15ml (1 tbsp) water
225g (8oz) pork, thinly sliced
225g (8oz) cake noodles
10ml (2 tsps) cornflour
Few drops sesame oil
Salt and freshly ground black pepper to taste
2.5ml (½ tsp) sugar
Oil

2 cloves of garlic, finely chopped
2.5cm (1 inch) fresh root ginger, peeled and sliced
2-3 spring onions, chopped
6 eggs, well beaten

Mix the bicarbonate of soda and the water together. Mix in the pork and marinate for 10-12 minutes. Drain. Cook the noodles in boiling, salted water for 3-4 minutes. Drain, rinse in cold water and drain once again. Toss in 15ml (1 tbsp) oil. Heat 30ml (2 tbsps) oil in the wok and brown the garlic. Add 5ml (1 tsp) salt and the noodles, and stir-fry for 3-4 minutes, until they turn light brown. Remove and keep on one side. Heat sufficient oil for deep frying in the wok and deep-fry the pork for 3-4 minutes, drain and remove. Tip off the oil. Heat 15ml (1 tbsp) oil in the wok. Add the ginger and onions and stir-fry for 1-2 minutes. Add the pork and then pour in the beaten eggs, mixing well. Add the cornflour, sesame oil and sugar and cook until the mixture thickens. Pour over the noodles and serve immediately.

Vegetable Rice

PREPARATION TIME: 10 minutes

COOKING TIME: 5-8 minutes

SERVES: 6-8 people

450g (1lb) rice, cooked
175g (6oz) Chinese leaves, shredded
100g (4oz) sliced green beans
100g (4oz) frozen peas
3 spring onions, chopped
15ml (1 tbsp) light soy sauce
Salt to taste

Rinse the cooked rice in cold water and drain. Put the moist rice into a pan. Arrange the Chinese leaves, sliced beans, peas and onions on top. Cover and cook over a gentle heat for 4-6 minutes. Sprinkle with soy sauce and add salt to taste. Stir the vegetables evenly into the rice and raise the heat for a few seconds. Serve immediately.

Fried Noodles with Shredded Chicken

PREPARATION TIME: 15 minutes

COOKING TIME: about 10 minutes

SERVES: 4 people

Oil
225g (8oz) cooked chicken, shredded
1 clove of garlic, chopped
2-3 spring onions, chopped
100g (4oz) whole green beans (or long Chinese beans, cut into 7.5cm (3-inch) pieces
450g (1lb) noodles, cooked until just tender
15ml (1 tbsp) cornflour
250ml (8 fl oz) chicken stock
15ml (1 tbsp) soy sauce
15ml (1 tbsp) oyster sauce
5ml (1 tsp) wine
5ml (1 tsp) sugar
1.25ml (¼ tsp) salt

Heat 30ml (2 tbsps) oil in a wok and cook the chicken for 2 minutes. Remove the chicken. Add the garlic, spring onions and beans and fry for 2 minutes. Remove the vegetables. Heat 30ml (2 tbsps) oil in the wok and toss the pre-boiled noodles over the heat for 2 minutes. Arrange on a plate and keep warm. Return the fried chicken, onion and green beans to the wok and stir-fry for 1 minute. Dissolve the cornflour in the chicken stock and add to the wok. Add the soy sauce, oyster sauce, wine, sugar, and salt and pepper to taste. Simmer until the sauce is thick. Pour over the bed of noodles and serve immediately.

Marbled Eggs

PREPARATION TIME: 10 minutes

COOKING TIME: 1 hour 10 minutes to 1 hour 15 minutes

MAKES: 6-8

These are eaten cold, dipped in a sauce, as a starter or a snack. Allow 1 egg per person.

6-8 eggs
45ml (3 tbsps) tea leaves
2.5cm (1 inch) cinnamon stick
2-3 star anise
30ml (2 tbsps) dark soy sauce
30ml (2 tbsps) light soy sauce

Boil the eggs for 8-10 minutes, until hard boiled. Drain and cool quickly by placing in iced water. Tap each egg shell with the back of a spoon until cracks appear all over. Bring enough water to the boil to cover the eggs. Add tea leaves, cinnamon, star anise and soy sauces, and stir. Add the eggs and simmer gently for at least 1 hour. Allow to cool and then shell before serving.

Eight Precious Rice

PREPARATION TIME: 20 minutes

MICROWAVE COOKING TIME: 10 minutes plus 2 minutes standing time

SERVES: 4 people

45ml (3 tbsps) oil
120g (4oz) chicken, cut in 1.25cm (½ inch) cubes
120g (4oz) frozen peas
60g (2oz) prawns
30g (1oz) diced bamboo shoots
8 water chestnuts, sliced thinly
60g (2oz) mushrooms, sliced thinly
4 spring onions, chopped
225g (8oz) cooked rice
2 eggs, beaten
30ml (2 tbsps) soy sauce
Salt and pepper

Heat oil in a large bowl 1 minute on HIGH. Add the chicken and cook, stirring frequently, for 3 minutes on HIGH. Cover the bowl loosely. Add the rice and cook 5 minutes on HIGH to heat through. Add the remaining ingredients and cook 1 minute on HIGH. Leave to stand, covered, 2 minutes before serving.

Deep Fried Noodles

Boil noodles for 5 minutes. Drain thoroughly on absorbent paper. Deep-fry in hot oil until crisp and golden.

Fried Rice Noodles

PREPARATION TIME: 25 minutes

COOKING TIME: 10 minutes

SERVES: 4-6 people

450g (1lb) rice noodles
45ml (3 tbsps) oil
100g (4oz) cooked chicken, shredded
50g (2oz) peeled shrimp
50g (2oz) bamboo shoots, sliced
2 sticks celery, chopped
50g (2oz) leek, chopped
2 spring onions, shredded
60ml (4 tbsps) stock
30ml (2 tbsps) soy sauce

Soak the rice noodles in warm water for 10-15 minutes. Drain thoroughly. Heat half the oil in a wok. Add the chicken, shrimp, bamboo shoots, celery, leeks and spring onions and stir-fry for 2-3 minutes. Add the stock, and salt and pepper to taste. Simmer for 2 minutes and then drain the chicken and vegetables. Heat the remaining oil, add the rice noodles and stir over the heat for 1 minute. Add the soy sauce and stir into the chicken-and-vegetable mixture. Cook together for 2-3 minutes. Serve immediately.

Assorted Meat Congee

PREPARATION TIME: 20 minutes

COOKING TIME: 1 hour 45 minutes

SERVES: 6 people

450g (1lb) rice
Scant 2.5 litres (4 pints) chicken stock
100g (4oz) tripe, well washed and chopped (optional)
100g (4oz) pig's or lamb's liver, sliced
100g (4oz) cooked beef, ham, lamb, chicken or pork, chopped
100g (4oz) whitefish fillets, thinly sliced
5ml (1 tsp) sesame oil
3 spring onions, chopped
7.5ml (1½ tsp) salt, or to taste
7.5ml (1½ tsp) freshly ground black pepper
1.25cm (½ inch) fresh root ginger, peeled and sliced

Wash the rice well and put it into a large saucepan. Add the chicken stock and the tripe (if used). Cook gently for 1-1½ hours or until the tripe is well cooked and the rice has become a soft pulp. In a separate saucepan, boil the sliced liver for 5 minutes in water. Drain and add to the rice. Add the cooked meat, fish, sesame oil, half the onions, salt and pepper and the slices of ginger. Cook for further 10-15 minutes, covered. Pour into large bowls and serve topped with the remaining chopped onions.

Rice Supreme

PREPARATION TIME: 10 minutes

COOKING TIME: 15 minutes

SERVES: 6 people

45ml (3 tbsps) cooking oil
15ml (1 tbsp) light soy sauce
2 eggs, beaten
1 small onion, peeled and finely sliced
50g (2oz) shrimp, peeled
50g (2oz) prawns, peeled
50g (2oz) whitefish, cubed
2 spring onions, finely chopped
50g (2oz) green pepper, seeded and cut into strips
450g (1lb) rice, cooked and cooled

Salt to taste
5ml (1 tsp) freshly ground black pepper
45ml (3 tbsp) tomato ketchup
50g (2oz) frozen peas

Heat 15ml (1 tbsp) oil in the wok and pour in the beaten eggs. Cook to make a thin omelette. Cut into thin strips. Heat 15ml (1 tbsp) oil in the wok and stir-fry the onion for 2 minutes. Add the shrimp, prawns and fish, and stir-fry for 3-4 minutes. Remove the fish mixture to a plate. Heat the remaining oil in the wok. Add half the spring onions and the green pepper, and stir-fry for 2 minutes. Add the rice and season with salt and pepper. Add the tomato ketchup, peas, fried fish, prawns and shrimp. Add the soy sauce and stir-fry for 3 minutes. Serve with the egg strips arranged on top of the rice. Sprinkle with the remaining spring onion.

Above: Deep-Fried Noodles (top), Stir-Fried Shanghai Noodles (page 44) (centre) and Fried Rice Noodles (bottom).

Noodles with Beef and Almonds

PREPARATION TIME: 15 minutes

COOKING TIME: 10 minutes

SERVES: 4 people

45ml (3 tbsps) oil
1 onion, chopped
4 cloves of garlic, chopped
2.5cm (1 inch) fresh root ginger, peeled and sliced
225g (8oz) beef, thinly sliced
50g (2oz) carrots, diced
50g (2oz) sliced green beans
50g (2oz) water chestnuts, sliced
50g (2oz) mushrooms, sliced
2 green chillies, sliced in half
Salt
5ml (1 tsp) sugar
5ml (1 tsp) monosodium glutamate (optional)
250ml (8 fl oz) chicken stock
100g (4oz) blanched almonds
450g (1lb) noodles, cooked until just tender

Heat 30ml (2 tbsps) oil in a wok. Fry the onion, garlic, ginger and beef for 3 minutes. Add the carrots and green beans and fry for 2 minutes. Add the water chestnuts, mushrooms and green chillies and fry for 1 minute. Add salt, sugar, monosodium glutamate and stock. Simmer for 1 minute. Remove to a dish and keep warm. Clean the wok and add the remaining oil. Fry the almonds and noodles for 1-2 minutes. Mix with the cooked vegetables and season with the soy sauce. Serve immediately.

Plain Fried Rice

PREPARATION TIME: 5 minutes, plus cooking time

COOKING TIME: 10-11 minutes

SERVES: 4-6 people

450g (1lb) Patna or long-grain rice
1.25ml (¼ tsp) monosodium glutamate
30ml (2 tbsps) oil
Salt

Wash the rice in 4-5 changes of cold water. Drain the rice and put into a large pan or wok. Add sufficient cold water to come 2.5cm (1 inch) above the level of the rice. Bring to the boil. Stir once and reduce the heat to simmer. Cover and cook for 5-7 minutes until the water has been totally absorbed and the rice is separate and fluffy, with the necessary amount of stickiness to be handled by chopsticks. (If necessary, cook for a little longer.) Spread the rice out on a tray and cool. Sprinkle with the monosodium glutamate. Heat the oil in a wok or large frying pan and add the rice. Stir-fry for 1-2 minutes. Add salt to taste and stir-fry for a further 1-2 minutes.

Stir Fried Shanghai Noodles

PREPARATION TIME: 10 minutes

COOKING TIME: 5-6 minutes

SERVES: 4 people

100g (4oz) white cabbage, shredded
2.5ml (½ tsp) sesame oil
45ml (3 tbsps) cooked oil
100g (4oz) cooked chicken or pork, shredded
450g (1lb) thick Shanghai noodles, cooked until just tender
30ml (2 tbsps) soy sauce
2.5ml (½ tsp) monosodium glutamate (optional)
Freshly ground black pepper to taste

Cook the cabbage in boiling water for 1 minute. Drain thoroughly. Heat the oils in a wok. Add the meat and stir-fry for 2-3 minutes. Add the cooked noodles, soy sauce, monosodium glutamate, and salt and pepper to taste. Add the cabbage, heat through and serve immediately.

Egg Noodles with Meat Sauce

PREPARATION TIME: 15 minutes

COOKING TIME: 20-22 minutes

SERVES: 4-6 people

45ml (3 tbsps) oil
3 cloves garlic, chopped
2.5cm (1 inch) fresh root ginger, peeled and shredded
1 onion, chopped
1 green pepper, seeded and sliced
450g (1lb) minced beef
2.5ml (½ tsp) salt
10ml (2 tsps) tomato purée
15ml (1 tbsp) soy sauce
2.5ml (½ tsp) freshly ground black pepper
120ml (4 fl oz) chicken stock
5ml (1 tsp) cornflour
450g (1lb) egg noodles
2 spring onions, chopped

Heat 30ml (2 tbsps) oil in a wok. Fry the garlic and ginger for 1-2 minutes. Add the onion and fry for 2-3 minutes. Add the green pepper and the minced beef and fry for 1 minute. Add half the salt, tomato purée, soy sauce and ground pepper. Fry for a further 3 minutes. Blend the stock and cornflour and add to the wok. Cook until thickened and the meat is tender. Meanwhile, cook noodles in boiling, salted water for 3-4 minutes, and drain. Rinse in cold water and drain once again. Heat the remaining oil in a pan. Add the noodles and toss over the heat until heated through. Arrange on a plate and top with the meat sauce. Garnish with chopped spring onions.

Shanghai Noodle Snack

PREPARATION TIME: 15 minutes

MICROWAVE COOKING TIME:
5-6 minutes plus 5 minutes standing time

SERVES: 6 people

450g (1lb) Chinese egg noodles
1150ml (2 pints) boiling water

SAUCE
30ml (2 tbsps) cornflour dissolved in 60ml (4 tbsps) water
30ml (2 tbsps) rice wine
15ml (1 tbsp) light soy sauce
280ml (½ pint) light stock
1 small piece ginger root, thinly sliced
4 spring onions, thinly sliced diagonally
Meat from one large crab or 1 180g (6oz) package frozen or canned crabmeat

Cook the noodles in the boiling water for 3 minutes on HIGH. Leave to stand 5 minutes, covered, while preparing the sauce. Combine the first 5 ingredients in a deep bowl, stirring well to mix the cornflour. Cook 2-3 minutes until the sauce thickens and clears. Add the crab and onion and cook for 30 seconds on HIGH. Drain the noodles well and toss with the sauce to serve.

Rice with Minced Beef

PREPARATION TIME: 10 minutes

COOKING TIME: 25 minutes

SERVES: 6 people

30ml (2 tbsps) cooking oil
225g (8oz) minced beef
3 spring onions, chopped
1.25cm (½ inch) fresh root ginger, peeled and sliced
2 cloves garlic, peeled and sliced
15ml (1 tbsp) soy sauce
1 green pepper, seeded and chopped
450g (1lb) rice, thoroughly washed
2.5ml (½ tsp) salt
5ml (1 tsp) freshly ground black pepper, or to taste

Heat the oil and fry the meat, onions, ginger and garlic for 5 minutes. Add the soy sauce and green pepper, and fry for 5-6 minutes. Cook the rice with 2.5cm (1 inch) water above the rice level with the salt for 5-6 minutes, or until the rice is semi-cooked and the water is almost absorbed. Spread the mince evenly over the rice. Cover and cook for 6-8 minutes over a very gentle heat. Remove and serve well mixed. Season with salt and pepper to taste.

Dumpling Wrappers

PREPARATION TIME: 50-60 minutes

MAKES: 40-45 wrappers

275g (10oz) plain flour
200ml (⅓ pint) cold water

Sieve the flour into a bowl and add the cold water, a little at a time, and mix to a firm dough. Knead the dough on a flat surface for 4-5 minutes. Cover with a damp cloth or wrap in cling film. Leave to stand at room temperature for 30-40 minutes. Roll out on a well-floured surface as thinly as possible, until almost transparent. Cut into round or square pieces to suit your requirements. Use within a few hours of making otherwise they will dry out.

Facing Page: Shanghai Noodle Snack.

FISH AND SEAFOOD

Sweet and Sour Fish

PREPARATION TIME: 15 minutes

MICROWAVE COOKING TIME: 11-13 minutes

SERVES: 4 people

4 trout, cleaned and trimmed
30ml (2 tbsps) sherry
1 small piece ginger root, peeled and sliced
120g (4oz) brown sugar
30g (2 tbsps) cornflour
90ml (3 fl oz) vinegar
30ml (2 tbsps) light soy sauce
2 carrots, thinly sliced
1 clove garlic, minced
2 spring onions, sliced
Salt and pepper

Place the trout in a shallow dish with the sherry, ginger and enough water to just cover the fish. Cover the dish with pierced cling film and cook 8-9 minutes on HIGH. Remove the fish to a serving dish and peel off the skin from one side. Cover and keep warm. Reserve the cooking liquid from the fish. Combine the remaining ingredients, except the spring onions and carrots, in a deep bowl. Cook for 2-3 minutes on HIGH or until the sauce thickens and clears. Thin the sauce with some of the fish cooking liquid until of thick coating consistency. Add the carrots and onions and cook 1 minute on HIGH. Pour over some of the sauce to serve with the fish, and serve the rest of the sauce separately.

This page: Sweet and Sour Fish. Facing page: Singapore Fried Noodles (top) and Steamed Fish with Black Beans (page 48) (bottom).

Singapore Fried Noodles

PREPARATION TIME: 20 minutes

COOKING TIME: 25 minutes

SERVES: 4 people

225g (8oz) packet egg noodles
225g (8oz) prawns, shelled and de-veined
1 chicken breast, cut into shreds
115g (4oz) bean sprouts
2 cloves garlic, crushed
3 sticks celery, sliced diagonally
2 spring onions, sliced
1 red chilli, seeds removed and sliced
1 green chilli, seeds removed and sliced
1 tsp chilli powder
2 eggs, lighty beaten
45ml (3 tbsps) oil
Salt
Pepper

GARNISH
Chilli flowers (carefully cut end of chilli into shreds, and soak in cold water until flower opens)

Soak noodles in boiling water for 8 minutes, or as directed. Drain noodles on absorbent paper and leave to dry. Heat wok, and add 15ml (1 tbsp) of oil. Add lightly beaten eggs, and salt and pepper to taste. Stir gently and cook until set. Remove from wok, cut into thin strips and keep warm. Add remaining oil to wok. When hot, add garlic and chilli powder and fry for 30 seconds. Add chicken, celery, spring onions and red and green chillies, and stir-fry for 8 minutes or until chicken has cooked through. Add noodles, prawns and bean sprouts, and toss until well mixed and heated through. Serve with scrambled egg strips on top and garnish with chilli flowers.

Prawns with Broccoli

PREPARATION TIME: 10 minutes

COOKING TIME: 8-10 minutes

SERVES: 4 people

450g (1lb) peeled prawns
Oil for deep frying

SAUCE
120ml (4 fl oz) chicken stock
10ml (2 tsps) cornflour
Freshly ground black pepper and salt to taste
Pinch monosodium glutamate (optional)
5ml (1 tsp) sugar

SEASONING
30ml (2 tbsps) cooked oil, or oil from deep frying the prawns
Pinch salt
2.5ml (½ tsp) sugar
Pinch monosodium glutamate (optional)
10ml (2 tsps) cornflour
250g (8oz) Chinese broccoli, or English broccoli, cut into 8cm (3-inch) pieces
1 carrot, peeled and sliced
2 cloves garlic, peeled and chopped
1cm (½ inch) fresh root ginger, peeled and chopped

Deep-fry the prawns in hot oil for 1-2 minutes. Drain the prawns and keep on one side. Retain the oil. Mix the sauce ingredients together. Mix the seasoning ingredients together in a separate bowl. Cook the broccoli in boiling water for 1 minute. Drain and add cold water to cover. Drain once again and mix the broccoli with the seasoning ingredients. Heat the wok, add 30ml (2 tbsps) cooked oil. Add the carrot, garlic and ginger and stir-fry for 1 minute. Add the broccoli and stir-fry for 1 minute more. Add the prawns and stir-fry for ½ minute then add the blended sauce ingredients. Cook gently until the sauce thickens. Serve immediately.

Prawns in Hot Sauce

PREPARATION TIME: 10 minutes

COOKING TIME: 6 minutes

SERVES: 4 people

350g (12oz) cooked, unshelled prawns

SEASONING
5ml (1 tsp) malt vinegar
5ml (1 tsp) Shao Hsing wine
Pinch salt

SAUCE
5ml (1 tsp) cornflour mixed with 15ml (1 tbsp) water
10ml (2 tsps) tomato purée
Salt and freshly ground black pepper to taste
10ml (2 tsps) sugar
2.5ml (½ tsp) monosodium glutamate (optional)
5ml (1 tsp) hot chilli sauce
180ml (6 fl oz) chicken stock
30ml (2 tbsps) cooked oil

Wash prawns and drain well. Mix the seasoning ingredients together. Mix the sauce ingredients together in a separate bowl. Heat the oil in a wok and deep-fry the prawns for 1 minute. Remove the prawns and drain. Keep the oil. Reheat the wok and add 10ml (2 tsps) oil and stir-fry the onion, celery and garlic for 1 minute. Add prawns and the blended sauce ingredients. Bring to the boil and simmer gently for 3-4 minutes. Stir in the seasoning mixture.

Steamed Fish with Black Beans

PREPARATION TIME: 15 minutes

COOKING TIME: 15 minutes

SERVES: 4 people

1kg (2lbs) whole snapper, bass or bream, cleaned and scaled
15ml (1 tbsp) salted black beans
2 cloves garlic, crushed
15ml (1 tbsp) light soy sauce
5ml (1 tsp) Chinese wine, or 10ml (2 tsps) dry sherry
5ml (1 tsp) sugar
2.5ml (½ tsp) cornflour
5ml (1 tsp) sesame oil
½ can bamboo shoots, cut into shreds

Prawns in Hot Sauce (right), Shrimp with Bean Curd (page 52) (centre right) and Prawns with Broccoli (bottom).

Salt
Pepper

Wash and clean fish well and dry with absorbent paper. Make 3 or 4 diagonal cuts in flesh of fish on each side. Rub garlic into cuts and place fish on a heat-proof dish. Rinse black beans in cold water, then crush with the back of a spoon. Add cornflour, sesame oil, soy sauce, sugar, wine, and salt and pepper and mix together well. Pour over fish. Sprinkle bamboo shoots on top of fish. Put plate on top of a bamboo steamer or metal trivet standing in wok. Add water, ensuring the level is below the level of the plate. Cover and bring to the boil. Steam for about 10 minutes after boiling point is reached. Ensure that the fish is cooked, but do not oversteam. Serve hot.

This page: Sesame Crab in Asparagus Ring. Facing page: Seafood Combination.

Seafood Combination

PREPARATION TIME: 20 minutes

COOKING TIME: 20 minutes

SERVES: 4 people

225g (8oz) prawns or shrimp, shelled and de-veined
115g (4oz) squid, cleaned, cut into 2.5cm (1-inch) rings, opened up, and scored with lattice design
115g (4oz) mangetout, trimmed
115g (4oz) whitefish fillet, cut into 2.5cm (1-inch) cubes

1 stick celery, sliced diagonally
1 carrot, scraped and cut into matchstick strips
5ml (1 tsp) grated root ginger
2.5ml (½ tsp) salt
15ml (1 tbsp) dry white wine
1 egg white
5ml (1 tsp) cornflour
Oil for deep frying

Combine wine, salt, egg white, grated ginger and cornflour, and mix well. Add prawns and fish, and toss well. Drain prawns and fish, reserving sauce. Blanch mangetout in boiling water for 1 minute. Drain. Heat oil in wok. Deep-fry prawns, fish and squid for 2 minutes. Remove from pan and drain on absorbent paper. Carefully remove oil from wok, reserving 15ml (1 tbsp) of oil in wok. Heat oil. Stir-fry carrot and celery for 3 minutes. Add mangetout and stir-fry a further 3 minutes. Add any remaining sauce and stir. Add seafood and toss well until heated through.

Sesame Crab in Asparagus Ring

PREPARATION TIME: 20 minutes

MICROWAVE COOKING TIME: 9-10 minutes

SERVES: 4 people

45ml (3 tbsps) sesame paste (tahini)
30ml (2 tbsps) light soy sauce
120ml (4 fl oz) light stock
30ml (2 tbsps) sherry
15ml (1 tbsp) cornflour
30ml (2 tbsps) Szechwan peppercorns
30ml (2 tbsps) oil
450g (1lb) asparagus, fresh or frozen, cut on the diagonal into 5cm (2-inch) pieces
30ml (2 tbsps) Chinese parsley leaves, left whole
4 spring onions, thinly sliced or shredded
Salt
Pinch sugar (optional)
450g (1lb) crabmeat (including some pink claw meat)
Sesame seeds

Combine the first 6 ingredients in a deep bowl. Cook for 2-3 minutes on HIGH, until thick, and set aside. Heat a browning dish 5 minutes on HIGH. Pour in the oil and add the asparagus. Stir-fry on HIGH for 4 minutes. If further cooking is needed, cover the dish and cook 1 minute on HIGH. Add the Chinese parsley, spring onions and crabmeat to the reserved sauce.

Sweet and Sour Prawns

PREPARATION TIME: 20 minutes

MICROWAVE COOKING TIME: 4-5 minutes plus 2 minutes standing time

SERVES: 4 people

SAUCE
Double recipe Sweet and Sour Sauce
Use reserved pineapple juice made up to 570ml (1 pint) with more canned juice

1 large green pepper, cut in 2.5cm (1-inch) pieces
4 tomatoes, peeled and quartered
4 spring onions, cut in 2.5cm (1-inch) pieces
225g (8oz) can pineapple chunks, juice reserved
675g (1½lbs) shelled prawns, de-veined

Prepare the Sweet and Sour Sauce. Add the green pepper to the hot sauce and cook 1 minute on HIGH. Add the pineapple, tomatoes, onions, and prawns, and cover tightly. Leave to stand 3 minutes before serving. Serve with rice.

Shrimp with Beancurd

PREPARATION TIME: 10 minutes

COOKING TIME: 8 minutes

SERVES: 4 people

450g (1lb) peeled shrimp

SEASONING
5ml (1 tsp) light soy sauce
Pinch salt
5ml (1 tsp) sugar
5ml (1 tsp) cornflour
2.5cm (1 inch) fresh root ginger, peeled and finely chopped
30ml (2 tbsps) oil
1 clove of garlic, peeled and chopped
1 red chilli, chopped
2-3 beancurd cakes, cubed
60ml (4 tbsps) chicken stock
5ml (1 tsp) cornflour
30ml (2 tbsps) water

Mix the shrimp with the seasoning ingredients and half the ginger. Heat the oil and stir-fry the ginger and shrimp for 2 minutes. Add the garlic and fry for 1 minute. Add the chilli, cubed beancurd and stock. Simmer for 2-3 minutes. Mix the cornflour with the water and remaining crushed ginger and pour over the shrimp mixture. Simmer gently until the sauce thickens. Serve immediately.

This page: Kung Pao Prawns (top) and Crabmeat Egg Fu Yung, Cantonese (page 56) (bottom). Facing page: Sweet and Sour Prawns (top) and Scallops in Pepper Sauce (page 56) (bottom).

Kung Pao Prawns

PREPARATION TIME: 20 minutes

MICROWAVE COOKING TIME: 5 minutes plus 2 minutes standing time

SERVES: 4 people

450g (1lb) shelled king prawns, de-veined
5ml (1 tsp) chopped fresh ginger root
5ml (1 tsp) chopped garlic
Salt and pepper
1.25ml (¼ tsp) sugar
1 small onion, coarsely chopped
1 courgette cut into 1.25cm (½-inch) cubes
60g (2oz) roasted cashew nuts

SAUCE
15ml (1 tbsp) cornflour
120ml (4 fl oz) stock
60ml (4 tbsps) soy sauce
5ml (1 tsp) red bean paste (optional)
5ml (1 tsp) sesame oil
15ml (1 tbsp) Shao Hsing wine or rice wine

Combine the prawns, ginger, garlic, sugar, salt and pepper in a casserole dish. Cover and refrigerate for 20 minutes. Combine all the sauce ingredients and pour over the prawns. Cover and cook for 3 minutes on MEDIUM. Stir often and do not allow the prawns to overcook. Add the remaining ingredients and cook 2 minutes on HIGH. Leave to stand 2 minutes before serving. Serve with rice.

Fish Steamed on Lotus Leaves

PREPARATION TIME: 25 minutes

MICROWAVE COOKING TIME: 13-16 minutes

SERVES: 4 people

4 small fish such as red mullet or small trout
4 dried Chinese mushrooms, soaked 30 minutes in hot water
45g (3 tbsps) shrimp
30ml (2 tbsps) oil
4 rashers streaky bacon, diced
1 small piece fresh ginger root, sliced
4 spring onions, finely chopped
30ml (2 tbsps) soy sauce
280ml (½ pint) stock
30ml (2 tbsps) cornflour dissolved in 60ml (4 tbsps) of the mushroom liquid
Salt and pepper
Sliced lotus root or bamboo shoots, cut in thin strips
2-4 lotus leaves, depending on size

Trim the fins from the fish and trim the tails neatly. Set fish aside in the refrigerator until ready to cook. Heat a browning dish for 5 minutes on HIGH. Pour in the oil and add the bacon. Cook 1 minute until beginning to brown. Drain the mushrooms and the shrimp. Dice the mushrooms and add to the bacon along with the shrimp, onions and ginger. Cook a further 1 minute on HIGH or until bacon is crisp. Place 1 or 2 lotus leaves in the bottom of a large, shallow dish. Lay the fish on top and scatter over the bacon mixture. Cover the fish with the remaining lotus leaves and pour over the soy sauce and stock. Cover the dish and cook the fish on HIGH for 9-11 minutes. When the fish are cooked, remove them and the lotus leaves from the dish and keep warm. Add the cornflour to the fish cooking liquid and stir well. Add salt and pepper and cook for 2-3 minutes on HIGH, or until the sauce has thickened. Add the lotus root or bamboo shoots. Remove the top layer of lotus leaves and serve the fish on the bottom leaves with the sauce.

Fish in Wine Sauce

PREPARATION TIME: 20 minutes

COOKING TIME: 15 minutes

SERVES: 3-4 people

MARINADE
1.25ml (¼ tsp) salt
1 egg white
10ml (2 tsps) cornflour
5ml (1 tsp) wine vinegar
275–350g (10-12oz) mullet or carp fillet, cut into 5cm (2-inch) slices
Oil for deep frying
250ml (8 fl oz) chicken stock

SEASONING
Pinch monosodium glutamate (optional)
Pinch salt
Pinch freshly ground black pepper
5ml (1 tsp) sugar
10ml (2 tsps) cornflour
15ml (1 tbsp) water
1 cloud ear fungus, soaked and boiled for 2 minutes, and then chopped
2 dried Chinese mushrooms, soaked and sliced

Mix the marinade ingredients together. Marinate the fish in the marinade for 10 minutes. Heat a generous quantity of oil in the wok and deep-fry the fish pieces, a few at a time, until the flesh is white. Remove and drain the fish. Keep the oil for future use. Clean the wok. Add the chicken stock to the wok and bring to the boil. Simmer gently and stir in the seasoning ingredients. Simmer for a few seconds and then add the cornflour blended with the water. Add the fish and simmer until the sauce thickens. Add the fungus and mushrooms. Simmer for 1 minute. Serve immediately.

Fish with Vegetables and Bean Curd

PREPARATION TIME: 20 minutes

COOKING TIME: 15 minutes

SERVES: 4 people

4 squares bean curd, cut into 2.5cm (1-inch) squares

SAUCE B
15ml (1 tbsp) Shao Hsing wine
15ml (1 tbsp) dark soy sauce
15ml (1 tbsp) light soy sauce
10ml (2 tsps) sugar
Pinch salt
Pinch white pepper
900ml (1½ pints) chicken stock
225g (8oz) cod fillet, cut into 5cm (2-inch) slices

SEASONING FOR FISH A
2.5ml (½ tsp) salt
2.5ml (½ tsp) Shao Hsing wine
22.5ml (1½ tbsps) cornflour
45ml (3 tbsps) oil

SEASONING FOR CABBAGE C
2.5ml (½ tsp) sugar
Pinch salt
5ml (1 tsp) cornflour
2.5cm (1 inch) fresh root ginger, peeled and shredded
2 spring onions, chopped
22.5ml (1½ tbsps) cornflour mixed with 30ml (2 tbsps) water
25g (1oz) bean sprouts
Few slices of pepper, diced
1 small carrot, chopped
25g (1oz) shelled or frozen peas

Soak the bean curd in cold water for 2 minutes. Drain well. Mix the sauce B ingredients and keep on one side. Wash the fish and drain well. Mix seasoning A ingredients and marinate fish for 10-12 minutes. Heat the wok and add half the oil. When very hot, add the cabbage and seasoning C ingredients

Above: Fish Steamed on Lotus Leaves. Above right: Fish with Vegetables and Bean Curd (top), Fish in Wine Sauce (centre right) and Fish with Chicken and Vegetables (bottom).

and stir-fry for about 2 minutes. Drain the cabbage well. Discard any liquid. Heat wok and add the remaining oil. Add the ginger and onions and stir-fry for 1 minute. Add sauce B ingredients and bring to the boil. Add fish and boil for 1 minute. Add the bean curd and simmer over a low heat for 5-6 minutes. (The bean curd should become spongy to the touch.) Add the blended cornflour and water. Stir and simmer until the sauce thickens. Add the cabbage and simmer for a further 2 minutes. Serve immediately.

Fish with Chicken and Vegetables

PREPARATION TIME: 25 minutes

COOKING TIME: 15 minutes

SERVES: 4 people

450g (1lb) pomfret, plaice or lemon sole fillets, cut into 5cm (2-inch) pieces
225g (8oz) boned chicken, cut into 5cm (2-inch) slices
6 dried Chinese mushrooms, soaked and sliced
50g (2oz) button mushrooms, soaked and sliced
50g (2oz) button mushrooms, sliced
50g (2oz) bamboo shoots, sliced
50g (2oz) mustard green, kale or broccoli, or 4 asparagus tips
100g (4oz) mixed vegetables (peas, carrots, bean sprouts, etc)
1 small onion, peeled and sliced
5ml (1 tsp) salt
Cooked oil

MARINADE
1.25ml (¼ tsp) salt
5ml (1 tsp) white pepper
2.5ml (½ tsp) monosodium glutamate (optional)
10ml (2 tsps) cornflour
15ml (1 tbsp) cooked oil
1.25ml (¼ tsp) sesame oil

SAUCE
250ml (8 fl oz) chicken stock
Salt to taste
Freshly ground black pepper to taste
2.5ml (½ tsp) monosodium glutamate (optional)
10ml (2 tsp) cooked oil
5ml (1 tsp) lemon juice

Wash the fish and drain. Mix the marinade ingredients together and marinate fish for 10-15 minutes. Blanch the mustard green, kale or broccoli in boiling, salted water for 1 minute. Drain and keep on one side. Heat the wok with 15ml (1 tbsp) cooked oil and stir-fry the mixed vegetables and the onions for 2 minutes. Add the mustard green and stir-fry for 1 minute. Drain and remove onto a plate. Brush a deep plate with cooked oil and arrange the drained fish, mushrooms, chicken and bamboo shoots in alternate rows. Place the dish over a steamer. Cover and steam over boiling water for 7 minutes, until cooked. Remove the steamer from heat and keep on one side. Heat the wok and add the sauce ingredients and fish marinade. Bring to the boil and simmer for 1 minute, until thickened. Put the steamed fish, mushrooms etc. onto a serving plate and pour the hot sauce over the top. Serve immediately.

Cantonese Lobster

PREPARATION TIME: 30 minutes

MICROWAVE COOKING TIME: 5-6 minutes plus 1 minute standing time

SERVES: 4 people

1 560-675g (1¼-1½lb) cooked lobster
10ml (2 tsps) black beans soaked in 30ml (2 tbsps) water
4-6 dried Chinese mushrooms, soaked 30 minutes in hot water
10ml (2 tsps) soy sauce
140ml (¼ pint) light stock
60ml (4 tbsps) rice wine
1 clove garlic, minced
25ml (1½ tbsps) cornflour dissolved in 60ml (4 tbsps) mushroom soaking liquid
45ml (3 tbsps) chives
30g (1oz) mangetout
4 leaves Chinese leaves, cut into 2.5cm (1-inch) strips
45g (1½ oz) bean sprouts
5 water chestnuts, sliced
Salt and pepper

Combine the soy sauce, stock, wine and cornflour. Cook in a deep bowl for 2-3 minutes on HIGH, or until the sauce thickens. If it is too thick, add more of the mushroom soaking liquid. Drain and slice the Chinese mushrooms and add to the sauce with the black beans, slightly crushed. Remove the tail and claw meat from the lobster and as much of the leg meat as possible. Cut the meat into 1.25cm (½ inch) pieces, leaving the claws whole if desired. Add the vegetables to the sauce and cook 2 minutes on HIGH. Stir in the lobster and leave covered for 1 minute before serving. Use the whole claws without their shells as garnish, if desired.

Scallops in Pepper Sauce

PREPARATION TIME: 20 minutes

MICROWAVE COOKING TIME: 13-15 minutes

SERVES: 4 people

450g (1lb) scallops, shelled and cleaned, roe attached if possible
½ clove garlic, finely chopped
45ml (3 tbsps) rice wine
45ml (3 tbsps) light soy sauce
15ml (1 tbsp) cornflour dissolved in 90ml (3 fl oz) light stock
60ml (4 tbsps) sweet chilli sauce
1 small piece fresh ginger root, peeled and chopped
1 green pepper, thinly sliced
4 spring onions, sliced or shredded
Pinch sugar
Salt and pepper

If the scallops are large, cut in half, horizontally. Place in a casserole dish with the garlic, wine, soy sauce, sugar and salt and pepper. Cover the dish and cook for 10 minutes on MEDIUM. Remove the scallops and keep warm. Add the cornflour and stock to the hot cooking liquid and stir well. Add the chilli sauce and ginger root and cook 2-3 minutes, or until thickened. Add the green pepper and onions to the sauce and return the scallops to the dish. Cook 1-2 minutes on HIGH, until the scallops are cooked and the vegetables are still crisp. Serve with rice.

Crabmeat Egg Foo Yung, Cantonese

PREPARATION TIME: 20 minutes

MICROWAVE COOKING TIME: 10-13 minutes

SERVES: 4 people

6 eggs
225g (8oz) crabmeat
2 sticks celery, thinly sliced
6 large mushrooms, thinly sliced
60g (2oz) bean sprouts
½ onion, thinly sliced
5ml (1 tsp) sherry
Salt and pepper
30ml (2 tbsps) oil

SAUCE
15ml (1 tbsp) cornflour
5ml (1 tsp) sugar
280ml (8 fl oz) chicken stock
10ml (2 tsps) soy sauce
5ml (1 tsp) sherry
5ml (1 tsp) sesame oil
2.5ml (½ tsp) ketchup
Salt

Heat a browning dish 5 minutes on HIGH. Beat the eggs and mix in the remaining ingredients, except the oil and those for the sauce. Add oil to the browning dish and spoon in 30ml (2 heaped tbsps) of the egg mixture at a time. Cook 2-4 patties at a time for 2-3 minutes on MEDIUM on the first side, turn over and cook 1-2 minutes on the other. Re-heat browning dish after each batch. Keep warm while making the sauce. Combine all the sauce ingredients in a deep bowl. Cook uncovered 2-3 minutes on HIGH or until the sauce thickens and clears. Pour over the Egg Foo Yung to serve.

Cantonese Prawns

PREPARATION TIME: 10 minutes

COOKING TIME: 15 minutes

SERVES: 4 people

45ml (3 tbsps) oil
2 cloves garlic, finely crushed
450g (1lb) peeled prawns
5cm (2 inches) root ginger, peeled and finely chopped
100g (4oz) uncooked pork or bacon, finely chopped

SAUCE
15ml (1 tbsp) rice wine or dry sherry
15ml (1 tbsp) light soy sauce

Facing page: Cantonese Lobster.

5ml (1 tsp) sugar
250ml (8 fl oz) stock or water
15ml (1 tbsp) cornflour mixed with 30ml (2 tbsps) stock or water
2-3 spring onions, chopped
2 eggs, lightly beaten

Heat 15ml (1 tbsp) oil in a wok. Add the garlic and fry for 1 minute. Add the prawns and stir-fry for 4-5 minutes. Remove to a dish and keep warm. Add the remaining oil to the wok and fry the ginger and pork for 3-4 minutes, until it loses its colour. Add the mixed sauce ingredients to the wok and cook for 1 minute. Add the onions and cook for 1 minute. Add the beaten eggs and cook for 1-2 minutes, without stirring, until it sets. Spoon the egg mixture over the prawns. Alternatively, add the prawns along with the beaten eggs. Allow the eggs to set and then mix gently. Serve at once.

This page: Prawns with Mangetout and Sweetcorn. Facing page: Prawns and Ginger (top), Boiled Prawns (centre) and Cantonese Prawns (page 56) (bottom).

Boiled Prawns

PREPARATION TIME: 5 minutes, plus 10 minutes for the sauce

COOKING TIME: 10-15 minutes

SERVES: 6 people

SAUCE
30ml (2 tbsps) dark soy sauce
45ml (3 tbsps) light soy sauce
1cm (½ inch) fresh root ginger, peeled and shredded
2 spring onions, finely chopped
1 red chilli, seeded and shredded
60ml (4 tbsps) cooked oil
10ml (2 tsps) tomato purée

1kg (2lb) medium or large uncooked prawns in their shells
Salt

Mix the sauce ingredients together. Wash the prawns and drain. Place the prawns in a wire basket and lower into a large pan of boiling salted water. Boil for 10-12 minutes. Drain. Serve the drained hot prawns with small bowls of sauce for dipping.

Prawns and Ginger

PREPARATION TIME: 10 minutes

COOKING TIME: 10 minutes

SERVES: 4-6 people

30ml (2 tbsps) oil
675g (1½lb) peeled prawns
2.5cm (1 inch) fresh root ginger, peeled and finely chopped
2 cloves garlic, peeled and finely chopped
2-3 spring onions, chopped lengthways into 2.5cm (1-inch) strips
1 leek, white part only, cut into strips
100g (4oz) shelled peas
175g (6oz) bean sprouts

SEASONING
30ml (2 tbsps) dark soy sauce
5ml (1 tsp) sugar
Pinch monosodium glutamate (optional)
Pinch of salt

Heat the oil in a wok and stir-fry the prawns for 2-3 minutes. Remove the prawns to a dish. Reheat the oil and add the ginger and garlic and fry for 1 minute. Add the onions and stir-fry for

1 minute. Add the leek, peas and bean sprouts. Stir-fry for 2-3 minutes. Sprinkle over the seasoning ingredients and return the prawns to the wok. Cover and cook for 2 minutes. Serve immediately.

Prawns with Mangetout and Sweetcorn

PREPARATION TIME: 20 minutes

MICROWAVE COOKING TIME: 5-8 minutes

SERVES: 4 people

675g (1½lbs) shelled king prawns, uncooked
45ml (3 tbsps) oil
1 clove garlic, minced
1 small piece ginger root, minced
60ml (4 tbsps) light stock
60ml (4 tbsps) light soy sauce
60ml (4 tbsps) rice wine
10ml (2 tsps) cornflour
30ml (2 tbsps) Chinese parsley
60g (2oz) mangetout
120g (4oz) baby ears of corn
Salt

Heat a browning dish for 5 minutes on HIGH. Shell and de-vein the prawns if necessary. Add the oil to the dish and the prawns. Add the garlic and ginger and cook for 1-2 minutes on HIGH, stirring often. Combine the stock, soy sauce, wine and cornflour. Pour over the prawns and cook for 3-4 minutes on MEDIUM, stirring halfway through the cooking time. Cut the stalks off the mangetout and add with the ears of corn to the dish. Cut the corn in half lengthwise if the ears are large. Cook for 1-2 minutes on MEDIUM, until the sauce thickens and clears. If the prawns are cooked after 3-4 minutes, remove them before adding the vegetables. Serve with rice or noodles.

Prawns with Peas

PREPARATION TIME: 15 minutes

MICROWAVE COOKING TIME: 3 minutes plus 2 minutes standing time

SERVES: 4 people

This page: Shrimp and Cauliflower (page 63) (top right), Prawns with Cashew Nuts (centre left) and Snow Peas with Shrimp (page 63) (bottom).

675g (1½ lbs) shelled king prawns
15ml (1 tbsp) cornflour
30ml (2 tbsps) rice wine
90ml (3 fl oz) light stock
30ml (2 tbsps) light soy sauce
Dash sesame oil
120g (4oz) frozen peas

Shell and de-vein the prawns and set aside. Combine the remaining ingredients, except the peas, in a deep bowl. Cook for 2-3 minutes on HIGH, or until the sauce thickens, stirring after 1 minute. Add the prawns, lower the setting to MEDIUM and cook for about 3 minutes. Check the prawns after 2 minutes – they must not overcook or they will toughen. Add the frozen peas during the last 1 minute of cooking. Add salt if necessary and serve with rice or noodles.

Prawns with Cashew Nuts

PREPARATION TIME: 10 minutes

COOKING TIME: 7-8 minutes

SERVES: 4 people

45ml (3 tbsps) oil
50-75g (2-3oz) cashew nuts
10ml (2 tsps) cornflour
250ml (8 fl oz) chicken stock or water
1 onion, peeled and cut into small pieces
25g (1oz) sliced green beans
50g (2oz) Chinese cabbage or white cabbage, shredded
50g (2oz) bamboo shoots, sliced
450g (1lb) peeled prawns
Salt and freshly ground black pepper to taste
4 rings pineapple, cut into chunks
Pinch monosodium glutamate (optional)

Heat 15ml (1 tbsp) oil in a wok and stir-fry the cashew nuts until light brown. Remove the nuts and keep on one side. Mix the cornflour with 30ml (2 tbsps) water or stock and keep on one side. Reheat the wok with the remaining oil and fry the onion for 1 minute. Add the beans, cabbage and bamboo shoots and stir-fry for 2-3 minutes. Add the cashew nuts and prawns and then add the remaining stock, salt and pepper, and the pineapple. Simmer for 1 minute and then add the monosodium glutamate and cornflour mixture and cook until the sauce thickens. Serve immediately.

Pineapple Prawns with Peppers

PREPARATION TIME: 20 minutes

MICROWAVE COOKING TIME: 6-7 minutes

SERVES: 4 people

SAUCE
Pineapple Sauce recipe (see page 150)
30ml (2 tbsps) rice wine
30ml (2 tbsps) light soy sauce
1 large green pepper, cut in thin strips
675g (1½ lbs) shelled king prawns, de-veined
45ml (3 tbsps) oil

Add the rice wine and soy sauce to the Pineapple Sauce recipe. If the sauce is still too thick, thin with a spoonful of water. Heat a browning dish 5 minutes on HIGH. Pour in the oil and add the prawns. Cook 1 minute on HIGH. Pour over the sauce, add the strips of pepper and cook 3 minutes on MEDIUM. Do not overcook or prawns will toughen. Serve with rice.

Crispy Fish with Chilli

PREPARATION TIME: 40 minutes

COOKING TIME: 30 minutes

SERVES: 4 people

450g (1lb) fish fillets, skinned, bones removed, and cut into 2.5cm (1-inch) cubes

BATTER
60g (2oz) plain flour
1 egg, separated
15ml (1 tbsp) oil
75ml (5 tbsps) milk
Salt

SAUCE
5ml (1 tsp) grated root ginger
1.25ml (¼ tsp) chilli powder
30ml (2 tbsps) tomato purée
30ml (2 tbsps) tomato chutney
30ml (2 tbsps) dark soy sauce
30ml (2 tbsps) Chinese wine or dry sherry
30ml (2 tbsps) water
5ml (1 tsp) sugar
1 red chilli, seeds removed, and sliced finely

1 clove garlic, crushed
Salt
Pepper
Oil for deep frying

Sift the flour with a pinch of salt. Make a well in the centre, and drop in the egg yolk and oil. Mix to a smooth batter with the milk, gradually incorporating the flour. Beat well. Cover and set aside in a cool place for 30 minutes. Whisk egg white until stiff, and fold into batter just before using. Heat oil in wok. Dip fish pieces into batter and coat completely. When oil is hot, carefully lower fish pieces in and fry until cooked through and golden brown – about 10 minutes. Remove with a slotted spoon. Reheat oil and refry each fish piece for 2 minutes. Remove with a slotted spoon and drain on absorbent paper. Carefully remove all but 15ml (1 tbsp) of oil from wok. Heat oil and add chilli, ginger, garlic, chilli powder, tomato purée, tomato chutney, soy sauce, sugar, wine, water, and salt and pepper to taste. Stir well over heat for 3 minutes. Increase heat and toss in fish pieces. Coat with sauce and, when heated through, serve immediately.

Shrimp and Cauliflower

PREPARATION TIME: 15 minutes

COOKING TIME: 14-15 minutes

SERVES: 4-6 people

45ml (3 tbsps) oil
1 clove of garlic, peeled and finely chopped
450g (1lb) shrimp, peeled
275g (10oz) cauliflower florets, cut into smaller pieces
250ml (8 fl oz) water or stock
Salt to taste
175g (6oz) shelled peas

SAUCE
10ml (2 tsps) cornflour
30ml (2 tbsps) stock or water
Freshly ground black pepper to taste

Heat the oil in a wok and fry the garlic for 2 minutes. Add the shrimp and cook for 3 minutes. Remove the shrimp. Add cauliflower and fry for 2-3 minutes, stirring constantly. Add stock, cover, and simmer for five minutes. Add salt to taste and the peas, and cook for a further 2-3 minutes. Return the shrimp to the wok and stir well. Add the blended sauce ingredients and simmer gently until it thickens. Serve immediately.

Facing page: Squid with Broccoli and Cauliflower (page 66). This page: Ginger Scallops in Oyster Sauce (page 64) (top) and Crispy Fish with Chilli (bottom).

Snow Peas with Shrimp

PREPARATION TIME: 10 minutes

COOKING TIME: 6-8 minutes

SERVES: 4-6 people

5ml (1 tsp) cornflour
5ml (1 tsp) sugar
5ml (1 tsp) dark soy sauce
15ml (1 tbsp) water
45ml (3 tbsps) oil
450g (1lb) peeled shrimp
180ml (6 fl oz) chicken stock
2.5ml (½ tsp) salt
100g (4oz) snow peas (mangetout)

75g (3oz) water chestnuts, sliced
1 small onion, peeled and cut into small pieces
1 stem celery, cut into 5mm (¼-inch) pieces
Pinch monosodium glutamate (optional)

Mix together the cornflour, sugar, soy sauce and water. Heat the oil in a wok. Add the shrimp, and stir-fry for 2 minutes. Add the stock, salt, snow peas, water chestnuts, onions and celery. Cover and cook for 2 minutes. Stir in the monosodium glutamate. Stir in the cornflour mixture and simmer gently until the sauce thickens. Serve as a side dish.

Ginger Scallops in Oyster Sauce

PREPARATION TIME: 10 minutes

COOKING TIME: 15 minutes

SERVES: 4 people

450g (1lb) scallops, cleaned, dried on absorbent paper, and sliced
10 spring onions, cut diagonally into 2.5cm (1-inch) slices
2.5cm (1 inch) green ginger, peeled and sliced very thinly
Salt
30ml (2 tbsps) vegetable oil

SAUCE
1 tbsp oyster sauce
15ml (1 tbsp) light soy sauce
2.5ml (½ tsp) sesame oil
5ml (1 tsp) grated root ginger
5ml (1 tsp) cornflour
75ml (5 tbsps) light stock, or 75ml (5 tbsps) hot water and half a chicken stock cube
Pinch of sugar

Combine oyster sauce, soy sauce, sesame oil, cornflour, sugar and grated ginger and set aside. Sprinkle the scallops with a pinch of salt. Heat wok, and add oil. Add sliced ginger and spring onions, and stir-fry gently for 1 minute. Raise heat to high. Add scallops and stir-fry for 1 minute. Add sauce mixture and stir in. Remove from heat, and stir in stock gradually. Return to heat and bring to the boil, stirring continously. Simmer gently for 3 minutes, until sauce is slightly thickened. Adjust seasoning. Serve immediately with boiled rice.

Steamed Fish in Ginger

PREPARATION TIME: 20 minutes

COOKING TIME: 15 minutes

SERVES: 4 people

1.5kg (3lb) whole snapper, bass or bream, cleaned and scaled

STUFFING
½ cup cooked rice
5ml (1 tsp) grated root ginger
3 spring onions, finely sliced
10ml (2 tsps) light soy sauce
6 spring onions, cut into 5cm (2-inch) lengths, then into fine shreds
3 pieces green ginger, cut into fine shreds

GARNISH
Lemon slices and parsley

Mix together rice, grated ginger, sliced spring onion and soy sauce. Stuff rice mixture into cleaned fish cavity, packing in well. Place fish on a heat-proof plate, and arrange strips of spring onion and green ginger on top of fish. Put the plate on top of a bamboo steamer or metal trivet standing in wok. Add water, ensuring the level is below the plate. Cover and bring to the boil. Steam for 10 minutes from boiling point. Ensure that the fish is cooked, but be sure not to oversteam the fish. Serve hot, garnished with lemon slices and parsley, if desired.

Honey Sesame Prawns

PREPARATION TIME: 20 minutes

COOKING TIME: 20 minutes

SERVES: 4 people

450g (1lb) prawns or shrimp, shelled and de-veined
30ml (2 tbsps) cornflour
115g (4oz) self-raising flour
1 egg, lightly beaten
Pinch of salt
Pepper
150ml (¼ pint) water
Oil for deep frying
30ml (2 tbsps) honey
15ml (1 tbsp) sesame seeds
15ml (1 tbsp) sesame oil

Sift flour and salt and pepper into a bowl. Make a well in the centre and add egg and water, gradually bringing in the flour. Beat to a smooth batter

Honey Sesame Prawns (top) and Steamed Fish in Ginger (right).

and set aside for 10 minutes. Meanwhile, toss prawns in cornflour and coat well, shaking off any excess. Add prawns to batter and coat well. Heat oil in wok, and add prawns, a few at a time. Cook until batter is golden. Remove, drain on absorbent paper, and keep warm. Repeat until all prawns have been fried. Carefully remove hot oil from wok. Gently heat sesame oil in wok. Add honey and stir until mixed well and heated through. Add prawns to mixture and toss well. Sprinkle over sesame seeds and again toss well. Serve immediately.

Squid with Broccoli and Cauliflower

PREPARATION TIME: 15 minutes

COOKING TIME: 20 minutes

SERVES: 4 people

450g (1lb) squid, cleaned
1 onion, peeled and chopped roughly
225g (8oz) fresh broccoli florets
225g (8oz) fresh cauliflower florets
2 sticks celery, sliced diagonally
2.5ml (½) tsp grated root ginger
15ml (1 tbsp) cornflour
30ml (2 tbsps) water
30ml (2 tbsps) light soy sauce
30ml (2 tbsps) Chinese wine, or dry sherry
30ml (2 tbsps) oyster sauce
2.5ml (½ tsp) sesame oil
2.5ml (½ tsp) sugar
150ml (¼ pint) oil, for deep frying
Salt
Pepper

Cut cleaned squid lengthways down centre. Flatten out with inside uppermost. With a sharp knife make a lattice design, cutting deep into squid flesh (to tenderise and make squid curl when cooking). Heat oil in wok. Add squid and cook until it curls. Remove from pan and drain on absorbent paper. Carefully pour off all but 15ml (1 tbsp) of oil. Add onion, celery, broccoli, cauliflower and ginger, and stir-fry for 3 minutes. Slake cornflour with water, and add soy sauce, wine, oyster sauce, sesame oil, sugar, and salt and pepper to taste. Mix well and add to wok. Bring to the boil and simmer for 3 minutes, stirring continously. Return squid and cook until heated through. Place in a warm serving dish and serve hot with rice.

Embroidered Crabmeat Balls

PREPARATION TIME: 25 minutes

MICROWAVE COOKING TIME: 5-6 minutes

SERVES: 4-6 people

450g (1lb) crabmeat
2-3 egg whites
5ml (1 tsp) salt
Pinch pepper
15ml (1 tbsp) sherry
15ml (1 tbsp) cornflour
½ green pepper, finely chopped
¼ red pepper, finely chopped
30ml (2 tbsps) finely chopped ham
2 spring onions, finely chopped
3 large leaves Chinese leaves, chopped
2.5ml (½ tsp) ground ginger
280ml (½ pint) hot chicken stock
30ml (2 tbsps) cornflour
30ml (2 tbsps) light soy sauce
Dash sesame oil

Mix together the first 12 ingredients, adding only 2 egg whites. If the mixture is dry and crumbly, add some of the remaining white until the mixture holds together. Shape into 2.5cm (1-inch) balls. The balls should not be smooth. Place in a single layer in a large, shallow dish. Pour around the hot stock and cover the dish. Cook 3 minutes on HIGH, rearranging the balls once during cooking to bring the ones in the centre of the dish to the outside. Remove the balls and keep warm. Mix the remaining cornflour with the soy sauce in a glass measure and gradually add the stock. Stir well and cook 2-3 minutes on HIGH, until thickened. Add the sesame oil and pour over the crabmeat balls to serve.

Squid with Prawns and Tomatoes

PREPARATION TIME: 25 minutes

MICROWAVE COOKING TIME: 4-5 minutes

SERVES: 4 people

225g (8oz) squid, cleaned
225g (8oz) prawns, peeled
30ml (2 tbsps) oil
180ml (6 fl oz) stock
30ml (2 tbsps) rice wine
15ml (1 tbsp) soy sauce
30ml (2 tbsps) tomato purée
15ml (1 tbsp) cornflour
1.25ml (¼ tsp) ground ginger
Salt and pepper
4 tomatoes, peeled and sliced

Heat the oil in a casserole dish for 30 seconds on HIGH. Cut the squid into rings and add to the oil with the prawns. Stir to coat and cook, covered, on MEDIUM for 2 minutes. Set aside. If using cooked prawns, add to the squid after 2 minutes. Combine all the sauce ingredients, except the tomatoes. Cook for 2-3 minutes on HIGH or until sauce has thickened. Add the tomatoes and pour over the squid. Leave to stand a few minutes to reheat the seafood. Serve with rice.

Facing page: Squid with Prawns and Tomatoes (top) and Embroidered Crabmeat Balls (bottom).

Chinese COOKING

MEAT DISHES

Beef with Broccoli

PREPARATION TIME: 20 minutes

MICROWAVE COOKING TIME: 7-8 minutes

SERVES: 4 people

450g (1lb) rump steak, cut in thin strips
45ml (3 tbsps) oil
60ml (4 tbsps) soy sauce
15ml (1 tbsp) cornflour
15ml (1 tbsp) sherry
5ml (1 tsp) sugar
90ml (3 fl oz) stock
½ bunch broccoli
10ml (2 tsps) grated ginger root
Salt and pepper

Heat a browning dish 5 minutes on HIGH. Mix the beef and oil and add to the dish. Cook 2 minutes on HIGH in 2 or 3 batches. Slice the stalks of the broccoli thinly on the diagonal. Separate the florets into small pieces. Toss in the oil with the meat and cook for 1 minute on HIGH. Leave to stand, covered, while preparing the sauce. Mix the soy sauce, cornflour, sherry, sugar and ginger root in a small bowl. Cook 2-3 minutes on HIGH, until thickened. Stir several times after 1 minute's cooking. Pour over the beef and broccoli. Cook a further 1 minute on HIGH. Adjust the seasoning and serve immediately with rice or noodles.

Sweet and Sour Pork with Pineapple

PREPARATION TIME: 20 minutes

COOKING TIME: 45 minutes

SERVES: 4 people

450g (1lb) lean pork fillet, cut into 2.5cm (1-inch) cubes
1 clove garlic, crushed
5ml (1 tsp) grated root ginger
30ml (2 tbsps) light soy sauce
15ml (1 tbsp) cornflour
30ml (2 tbsps) peanut oil
150ml (¼ pint) water
30ml (2 tbsps) white wine vinegar
30ml (2 tbsps) tomato purée
15ml (1 tbsp) sugar
1 can pineapple pieces, drained

GARNISH
Fresh coriander

Place pork in bowl. Pour over light soy sauce and toss together. Leave for 15 minutes. Make sauçe. Mix together vinegar, tomato purée and sugar, and set aside. Heat wok and add oil. Remove pork from soy sauce, and add soy sauce to sauce mixture. Toss pork in cornflour, coating well. When oil is hot, brown pork well on all sides. Remove from pan and reduce heat. Fry

This page: Beef with Broccoli. Facing page: Sweet and Sour Pork and Pineapple.

garlic and ginger for 30 seconds. Add water. Bring to the boil, then return pork to wok. Reduce heat, cover and simmer for 15 minutes, stirring occasionally. Add sauce mixture and pineapple, and simmer for a further 15 minutes. Garnish with coriander. Serve hot with rice or noodles.

Steak Chinese Style

PREPARATION TIME: 1 hour 15 minutes

COOKING TIME: 20 minutes

SERVES: 4 people

225g (8oz) fillet or rump steak, cut into 2.5cm (1-inch) pieces
1 can straw mushrooms, drained
2 spring onions, sliced diagonally into 1.5cm (½-inch) pieces
2 cloves garlic, crushed
1 can baby sweetcorn, drained
2.5ml (½ tsp) crushed ginger
15ml (1 tbsp) oyster sauce
15ml (1 tbsp) light soy sauce
30ml (2 tbsps) dark soy sauce
10ml (2 tsps) sugar
5ml (1 tsp) sesame oil
5ml (1 tsp) Chinese wine, or 10ml (2 tsps) dry sherry
5ml (1 tsp) cornflour
60ml (4 tbsps) water
Pinch of bicarbonate of soda
45ml (3 tbsps) peanut oil
Salt
Pepper

GARNISH
Spring onion flowers (cut spring onions into 5cm (2-inch) lengths. Carefully cut into fine shreds, keeping one end intact, and then soak in cold water until curling)

Put steak in a bowl and sprinkle over bicarbonate of soda. Mix together light soy sauce, sesame oil, wine, half the sugar, half the cornflour, and seasoning. Pour over the steak and leave for at least an hour, turning meat occasionally. Meanwhile, make sauce by mixing 30ml (2 tbsps) of dark soy sauce, remaining sugar and cornflour, and water. Mix together and set aside. Heat wok, add peanut oil and, when hot, fry steak for 4 minutes. Remove from wok and set aside. Add garlic, spring onions, ginger, mushrooms, baby sweetcorn, and finally steak. Add oyster sauce, mix well, then add sauce mixture and bring to the boil. Cook for 3 minutes, stirring occasionally. Serve hot with rice, garnished with spring onion flowers.

Beef with Pineapple and Peppers

PREPARATION TIME: 40 minutes

COOKING TIME: 15 minutes

SERVES: 4 people

450g (1lb) fillet or rump steak, thinly sliced
1 can pineapple slices, drained and chopped
1 green pepper, cored, seeds removed, and chopped roughly
1 red pepper, cored, seeds removed, and chopped roughly
2 cloves garlic, crushed
5ml (1 tsp) chopped root ginger
1 onion, peeled and chopped roughly
30ml (2 tbsps) light soy sauce
5ml (1 tsp) sugar
10ml (2 tsps) cornflour
30ml (2 tbsps) water
15ml (1 tbsp) peanut oil

SAUCE
15ml (1 tbsp) plum sauce
15ml (1 tbsp) dark soy sauce
5ml (1 tsp) sugar
5ml (1 tsp) sesame oil
1 tsp cornflour
60ml (4 tbsps) water
Salt
Pepper

Facing page: Steak Chinese Style. This page: Beef with Pineapple and Peppers.

Combine 30ml (2 tbsps) of light soy sauce with 1 tsp of sugar, 2 tsps of cornflour and 30ml (2 tbsps) water. Mix well and pour over steak. Toss together well, and put aside for at least 30 minutes, turning occasionally. Heat wok and add peanut oil. Add ginger, garlic, onion and peppers, and stir-fry for 3 minutes. Remove from wok and set aside. Add extra oil if necessary and stir-fry beef, well separated, for 2 minutes. Remove from wok. Mix together all sauce ingredients in wok, and heat until sauce begins to thicken. Add vegetables, beef and pineapple, and toss together over a high heat until warmed through. Serve with boiled rice.

Sliced Pork in Wine Sauce

PREPARATION TIME: 30 minutes

COOKING TIME: about 16 minutes

SERVES: 4 people

SEASONING

15ml (1 tbsp) red vinegar
15ml (1 tbsp) light soy sauce
15ml (1 tbsp) rice wine or dry sherry
10ml (2 tsp) soy paste
5ml (1 tsp) freshly ground black pepper
5ml (1 tsp) salt
5ml (1 tsp) Shao Hsing wine
450g (1lb) pork fillet, cut into 5cm (2-inch) long, thin slices
15ml (1 tbsp) cornflour
60ml (4 tbsps) oil
2.5cm (½ inch) fresh root ginger, finely chopped
3 spring onions, chopped
1 green pepper, seeded and diced

SAUCE

10ml (2 tsps) cornflour
60ml (4 tbsps) dry white wine
120ml (4 fl oz) chicken stock
10ml (2 tsps) dark soy sauce
5ml (1 tsp) sugar
2.5ml (½ tsp) salt

Mix the seasoning ingredients together. Add the pork slices and leave to marinate for 10-15 minutes. Drain the pork and roll in the cornflour. Leave on one side. Discard the marinade. Heat half the oil in the wok until smoking. Add the pork, reduce the heat, and stir-fry for 4-6 minutes, until lightly browned. Remove the pork and keep on one side. Discard any oil left in the wok. Add the remaining oil to the wok and stir-fry the spring onions, ginger and green pepper for 3-5 minutes. Return the fried pork to the wok and cook for a further 2-3 minutes with the vegetables. Remove onto a serving dish. Mix the cornflour from the sauce ingredients with 30ml (2 tbsps) water. Add the remaining sauce ingredients to the wok and bring to the boil. Add the blended cornflour. Stir and simmer until the sauce thickens, simmer for 1-2 minutes. Pour over the pork and serve.

Pork-Stuffed Mushrooms

PREPARATION TIME: 15-20 minutes

COOKING TIME: 12 minutes

SERVES: 4 people

FILLING

1 egg
10ml (2 tsps) cornflour
10ml (2 tsps) rice wine or dry sherry
1.25ml (¼ tsp) minced fresh root ginger
6 water chestnuts, finely chopped
50g (2oz) peeled shrimp, chopped
175g (6oz) lean pork, minced
1.25ml (¼ tsp) salt
1.25ml (¼ tsp) freshly ground black pepper
2.5ml (½ tsp) sugar
10ml (2 tsps) chilli sauce

16 large, open mushrooms
600ml (1 pint) chicken stock
Oil

Mix all the filling ingredients together. Remove the mushroom stalks. Divide the filling into 16 portions. Bring the

chicken stock to the boil. Add the mushrooms and leave to stand off the heat for 5 minutes, covered. Drain the mushrooms and discard the stock. Top each mushroom with a portion of filling. Put the stuffed mushrooms into a well-oiled steamer. Steam for 10-12 minutes over boiling water. Serve as a snack, as a starter or as a side dish. Alternatively, serve with a simple sauce made from thickened chicken broth. Pour the sauce over the steamed mushrooms.

Diced Pork with Sweetcorn (page 74) (far left), Sliced Pork in Wine sauce (left) and Pork-Stuffed Mushrooms (below).

Jade and Ivory Pork

PREPARATION TIME: 30 minutes

MICROWAVE COOKING TIME: 10-12 minutes

SERVES: 4 people

450g (1lb) pork fillet, cut in very fine strips
45ml (3 tbsps) oil
45ml (3 tbsps) yellow beans
60ml (4 tbsps) light soy sauce
30ml (2 tbsps) rice wine
15ml (1 tbsp) cornflour
180ml (6 fl oz) chicken stock
225g (8oz) can bamboo shoots, cut in strips if necessary
1 large green pepper, cut in strips about the same size as bamboo shoots

Heat a browning dish for 5 minutes on HIGH. Mix meat and oil and add to the dish. Cook for 2 minutes on HIGH, stirring often. Combine the yellow beans, soy sauce, wine, cornflour and stock. Mix very well and pour over the pork. Cover the dish or transfer to a covered casserole and cook for 5-7 minutes on MEDIUM, stirring halfway through the cooking time. Cook on HIGH for 2 minutes, until thickened. Add the pepper and bamboo shoots and cook a further 1 minute on HIGH. Serve with rice or noodles.

Diced Pork with Sweetcorn

PREPARATION TIME: 25 minutes

COOKING TIME: 15-20 minutes

SERVES: 2 people

MARINADE
Pinch salt
10ml (2 tsps) dark soy sauce
1.25ml (¼ tsp) sugar
5ml (1 tsp) rice wine
15ml (1 tbsp) water

175g (6oz) pork loin, diced
Oil for deep frying
2 slices fresh root ginger, peeled and diced
1 clove garlic, peeled and chopped
250ml (8 fl oz) chicken stock

SEASONING
1.25ml (¼ tsp) salt
1.25ml (¼ tsp) freshly ground black pepper
1.25ml (¼ tsp) sugar
5ml (1 tsp) rice wine or dry sherry
Few drops sesame oil
5ml (1 tsp) cornflour mixed with 15ml (1 tbsp) water

250ml (8 fl oz) creamed sweetcorn
1 egg, well beaten
4 spring onions, chopped

This page: Beef and Oyster Sauce (page 80). Facing page: Jade and Ivory Pork.

Mix the marinade ingredients together. Add the pork and leave to marinate for 15 minutes. Drain the pork and discard the liquid. Heat the wok and pour in the oil for deep frying. Fry the pork until light brown. Remove the pork and drain. Reserve the oil for future use. Heat 15ml (1 tbsp) oil in the wok, add the ginger and pork. Stir-fry for 3 minutes. Add the stock and simmer for 3 minutes. Add the seasoning ingredients and simmer for 2-3 minutes. Add the blended cornflour and water and simmer until the sauce thickens. Add the sweetcorn and beaten egg and cook for 2-3 minutes. Serve sprinkled with chopped onions. Serve this dish with plain boiled rice or noodles.

Pink and Silver Pork

PREPARATION TIME: 15 minutes

MICROWAVE COOKING TIME: 11-16 minutes

SERVES: 4 people

225g (8oz) pork fillet, cut into thin shreds
225g (8oz) ham, cut into thin strips
280ml (½ pint) light stock
60ml (4 tbsps) rice wine
30ml (2 tbsps) light soy sauce
1 clove garlic, finely minced
1 small piece fresh ginger root, grated
15ml (1 tbsp) cornflour mixed with 30ml (2 tbsps) water
120g (4oz) bean sprouts

Combine all the ingredients, except the bean sprouts, in a large casserole dish and cover. Cook for 10-15 minutes on MEDIUM, stirring halfway through the cooking time. Add the bean sprouts and cook a further 1 minute on HIGH. Leave to stand 2 minutes before serving.

Beef with Mango

PREPARATION TIME: 20 minutes

COOKING TIME: 15 minutes

SERVES: 4 people

450g (1lb) fillet or rump steak, thinly sliced
1 can mangoes, drained, reserving 60ml (4 tbsps) juice

5ml (1 tsp) sugar
2.5ml (½ tsp) salt
5ml (1 tsp) cornflour
Pinch of pepper
30ml (2 tbsps) mango chutney
15ml (1 tbsp) plum sauce
15ml (1 tbsp) oil

Combine 30ml (2 tbsps) mango juice, sugar, cornflour, salt and pepper, and pour over steak. Toss well and set aside for 15 minutes. Mix remaining mango juice with mango chutney and plum sauce, and set aside. Chop finely half of the mangoes and add to the sauce, retaining enough slices for decoration. Heat wok and add oil. Stir-fry steak for 5 minutes, tossing well, until browned all over. Add mango-plum sauce and cook for a further 5 minutes. Decorate dish with reserved mango slices. Serve with rice.

Pork in Plum Sauce with Almonds

PREPARATION TIME: 30 minutes

MICROWAVE COOKING TIME: 11-18 minutes

SERVES: 4 people

SAUCE
Plum Sauce recipe (see page 142)
1 purple or red plum, thinly sliced
450g (1lb) pork fillet, cut in thin slices

Facing page: Pink and Silver Pork (top) and Pork in Plum Sauce with Almonds (bottom). This page: Beef with Mango.

30ml (2 tbsps) oil
30ml (2 tbsps) soy sauce

GARNISH
60g (2oz) toasted whole almonds

When the plum sauce is ready, add the thinly-sliced plum, keep the bowl covered and set aside while preparing the pork. Heat a browning dish for 5 minutes on HIGH. Pour in the oil and add the pork. Cook for 2 minutes on HIGH, stirring often. Add the soy sauce, cover the dish and cook for 5-7 minutes more on MEDIUM. When the pork is tender, pour over the plum sauce and heat for 1 minute on HIGH. Serve sprinkled with the toasted almonds.

Pork Spare Ribs

PREPARATION TIME: 25 minutes

COOKING TIME: 40-45 minutes

SERVES: 4 people

16-20 spare ribs
5ml (1 tsp) salt
Oil
5ml (1 tsp) ginger paste
5ml (1 tsp) garlic paste
5ml (1 tsp) onion paste
Pinch monosodium glutamate (optional)
5ml (1 tsp) light soy sauce
5ml (1 tsp) cornflour
1 egg
2.5ml (½ tsp) Shao Hsing wine
2.5ml (½ tsp) chilli oil

SAUCE
45ml (3 tbsps) sugar
45ml (3 tbsps) black vinegar
15ml (1 tbsp) tomato ketchup (optional)
5ml (1 tsp) cornflour
5ml (1 tsp) water
15ml (1 tbsp) dark soy sauce
2.5ml (½ tsp) salt
2.5ml (½ tsp) freshly ground black pepper

Trim excess fat from spare ribs and rub with salt. Add 60ml (4 tbsps) oil to the wok and fry the ginger, garlic and onion pastes for 1-2 minutes. Add the spare ribs and stir-fry for 6 minutes. Remove to a dish and add the monosodium glutamate, light soy sauce, cornflour, egg, wine and chilli oil. Marinate for 10 minutes. Prepare the sauce by mixing all the ingredients together in the wok and bringing them gently to the boil. Simmer for 2-3 minutes and add the spare ribs along with their marinade. Stir-fry until the liquid is reduced to half its original volume. Put all the ingredients onto a baking tray and spread out evenly. Bake at 190°C, 375°F, Gas Mark 5, for 25 minutes. Baste occasionally with the liquid from the tray and the oil. The spare ribs should have browned well and be well coated with seasoning. Serve hot or cold.

Pork Meatballs in Sauce (left), Pork Spare Ribs (above) and Barbecued Pork (page 80) (right).

Pork Meat Balls in Sauce

PREPARATION TIME: 25 minutes

MICROWAVE COOKING TIME: 45 minutes

SERVES: 4 people

SEASONING

Pinch monosodium glutamate (optional)
15ml (1 tbsp) Shao Hsing wine
2cm (1 inch) fresh root ginger, peeled and minced
2 spring onions, white part only, minced
2.5ml (½ tsp) salt
10ml (2 tsps) cornflour
450g (1lb) lean pork, minced
25g (1oz) bamboo shoots, chopped
50g (2oz) dried Chinese mushrooms, soaked, drained and sliced
1 egg, beaten
Cornflour for dredging
175g (6oz) Chinese white cabbage, cut into 7.5cm (3-inch) pieces, or 225g (8oz) ordinary green leafy cabbage, cut into 7.5cm (3-inch) pieces
15ml (1 tbsp) cooked oil
Oil for deep frying
15ml (1 tbsp) cornflour
45ml (3 tbsps) water
1 small onion, peeled and finely chopped
2.5cm (1 inch) fresh root ginger, peeled and finely chopped
300ml (½ pint) chicken stock

SAUCE

Salt to taste
2.5ml (½ tsp) monosodium glutamate (optional)
15ml (1 tbsp) light soy sauce
5ml (1 tsp) dark soy sauce
15ml (1 tbsp) cooked oil

Mix seasoning ingredients together. Add the pork, bamboo shoots, mushrooms and egg, and mix well. Shape into 15-16 even-sized balls and roll them in cornflour. Keep aside on a dish. Blanch cabbage for 1 minute in boiling water and the cooked oil. Drain the cabbage and discard the water. Heat the wok and add the oil for deep frying. When quite hot, deep-fry the meat balls, a few at a time, for 4-5 minutes. Remove and drain. Keep warm in a large casserole dish. Keep oil for future use. Mix the 15ml (1 tbsp) cornflour with the 45ml (3 tbsps) water and keep aside. Reheat the wok and add 5ml (1 tsp) deep frying oil. Stir-fry the onion and ginger for 2 minutes. Add the chicken stock and stir in the blended sauce ingredients. Bring to the boil and add the meat balls. Simmer gently for 30 minutes. Add the cabbage, sesame oil and the blended cornflour mixture. Stir over the heat until the sauce thickens.

Beef with Tree Ears

PREPARATION TIME: 30 minutes

MICROWAVE COOKING TIME: 7-8 minutes

SERVES: 4 people

8 pieces dried black fungi (tree or wood ears)
450g (1lb) rump steak, cut in thin strips
45ml (3 tbsps) oil
60ml (4 tbsps) soy sauce
15ml (1 tbsp) rice wine
10ml (2 tsps) chilli sauce (sweet or hot)
90ml (3 fl oz) stock
15ml (1 tbsps) cornflour
1 small bunch chives, chopped

Soak the tree ears for 20 minutes in hot water. Heat a browning dish for 5 minutes on HIGH. Combine oil and meat and add to the dish. Cook 2 minutes on HIGH in 2 or 3 batches. Re-heat dish 2 minutes after each batch. Drain the tree ears well and add whole to the steak in the browning dish. Cook 1 minute on HIGH, turning once. Mix the remaining ingredients, except the chives, together and pour over the meat and tree ears. Cook 2-3 minutes on HIGH, until the sauce thickens and clears. Sprinkle over the chopped chives before serving.

Barbecued Pork

PREPARATION TIME: 3 hours

COOKING TIME: 1 hour to 1 hour 30 minutes

SERVES: 6-8 people

2kg (4½lb) loin of pork

SEASONING
15ml (1 tbsp) ginger juice
Few drops red food colouring
75ml (5 tbsps) sugar
180ml (6 fl oz) light soy sauce
5ml (1 tsp) salt
15ml (1 tbsp) Mue Kwe Lo wine (or a mixture of 10ml (2 tsps) dry sherry and 5ml (1 tsp) apricot brandy)

225g (½lb) honey, melted

Remove the bones from the loin of pork. Cut pork into 4cm (1½-inch) wide strips. With the aid of a fork, scrape the surface of the pork lightly to form grooves in which the seasoning can lodge. Mix the seasoning ingredients together and rub well into the pork strips. Leave to marinate for at least 1½ hours. Thread the pork strips onto a long metal skewer and hang to dry for 1 hour. Put the pork on a wire rack in a roasting tin. Brush with melted honey and roast in the oven 180°C, 350°F, Gas Mark 4, for 1-1½ hours, frequently basting with honey.

When cooked, brush the pork with any remaining honey and leave to 'dry' slightly. Serve hot or cold, sliced thinly, on a serving plate.

Steamed Beef Balls with Two Different Mushrooms

PREPARATION TIME: 30 minutes

MICROWAVE COOKING TIME: 11-14 minutes

SERVES: 4-6 people

20 dried Chinese mushrooms
340g (12oz) minced beef
45ml (3 tbsps) light soy sauce
10ml (2 tsps) dry sherry
10ml (2 tsps) grated fresh ginger root
Salt and pepper
24 fresh or frozen shelled peas
340-400g (12-14oz) Chinese straw mushrooms or small button mushrooms
30ml (2 tbsps) cornflour dissolved in 45ml (3 tbsps) water

Soak the dried mushrooms for 30 minutes in hot water. Combine the minced beef, half the soy sauce, sherry, ginger, salt and pepper, and shape into 24 small balls. Press one pea into the top of each beef ball. Arrange in a glass dish, with space between each ball if possible. Combine the remaining soy sauce with 280ml (½ pint) water. Pour over the beef balls and cover loosely with cling film. Cook on HIGH for 8-10 minutes. Turn the beef balls over to rearrange them once or twice during cooking. Make sure that those in the centre are brought to the outside of the dish. When the beef balls are cooked, remove to a serving dish and keep warm. Arrange in rows or in a circle, pea-side up. Skim the fat from the top of the cooking liquid. Combine the cornflour with a spoonful of liquid. Stir into the remaining liquid in the dish and mix well. Cook for 2-3 minutes on HIGH, stirring after 1 minute. Add the two different mushrooms and cook until the sauce thickens. Arrange the mushrooms on the serving dish, keeping the two different kinds separate. Pour over the sauce to serve.

Beef and Oyster Sauce

PREPARATION TIME: 30 minutes

COOKING TIME: 20 minutes

SERVES: 4 people

450g (1lb) fillet or rump steak, sliced into thin strips
115g (4oz) bean sprouts
115g (4oz) button mushrooms
1 red pepper, cored, seeds removed, and chopped roughly
2 sticks celery, sliced diagonally
2 onions, peeled and quartered
30ml (2 tbsps) light soy sauce
30ml (2 tbsps) peanut or vegetable oil

OYSTER SAUCE
3 tbsps oyster sauce
1 chicken stock cube dissolved in 30ml (2 tbsps) boiling water
15ml (1 tbsp) dark soy sauce
15ml (1 tbsp) Chinese wine or dry sherry
15ml (1 tbsp) cornflour
30ml (2 tbsps) cold water
Salt
Pepper

Place steak in a bowl and pour over 30ml (2 tbsps) light soy sauce. Toss together well and set aside for at least 30 minutes. Meanwhile, mix together oyster sauce, chicken stock, dark soy sauce and wine. Blend together cornflour and cold water, and set aside. Heat wok, and add oil. Add onion, celery, mushrooms and red pepper, and stir-fry for 5 minutes. Remove from wok and set aside. Reheat oil and, when

Facing page: Steamed Beef Balls with Two Different Mushrooms (top) and Beef with Tree Ears (bottom).

hot, toss in steak. Brown well all over, then add sauce and fried vegetables. Add cornflour mixture and bring to the boil, tossing continuously. Add salt and pepper to taste. Finally, add bean sprouts and simmer gently for 3 minutes. Serve hot with noodles or rice.

Steamed Beef Szechuan Style

PREPARATION TIME: 40 minutes

COOKING TIME: 15 minutes

SERVES: 4 people

3 slices fresh root ginger, minced
5ml (1 tsp) salt
5ml (1 tsp) sugar
Freshly ground black pepper
15ml (1 tbsp) oil
30ml (2 tbsps) rice wine or dry sherry
22.5ml (1½ tbsps) chilli bean paste
30ml (2 tbsps) dark soy sauce
3-4 spring onions, finely chopped
450g (1lb) fillet of beef, cut into 5cm (2-inch) long strips
100g (4oz) ground rice
1 large lotus leaf, or several cabbage leaves

For the marinade, mix together the ginger, salt, sugar, pepper, oil, wine, bean paste, soy sauce and half of the spring onions. Add beef strips and mix well. Leave to marinate for 15-20 minutes. Heat the wok and dry-roast the ground rice for 2-4 minutes, till rice changes colour from white to light brown. Roll the marinated beef in the roasted ground rice to give a thin, even coating. Line the bamboo steamer with a well-oiled lotus leaf or a few old and tough cabbage leaves. Arrange the coated beef strips in a neat pile on top. Steam fairly quickly for 10-15 minutes over boiling water. Garnish with the remaining chopped spring onions before serving. Serve hot with chilli sauce.

Steamed Pork with Salted Cabbage

PREPARATION TIME: 25 minutes

COOKING TIME: 2 hours

SERVES: 4 people

450g (1lb) fillet pork cut into 1cm (½-inch) thick slices
Salt
175g (6oz) cabbage, shredded (Chinese white or plain green cabbage)

SEASONING
15ml (1 tbsp) sugar
30ml (2 tbsps) cooked oil
5ml (1 tsp) monosodium glutamate (optional)
60ml (4 tbsps) stock or water
Salt and freshly ground black pepper

15ml (1 tbsp) dark soy sauce
Oil for deep frying

SAUCE
5ml (1 tsp) cornflour
15ml (1 tbsp) water

Boil the pork in 450ml (¾ pint) water for ¾ hour, until tender. Drain the pork and discard the water. Boil 450ml (¾ pint) fresh water with 5ml (1 tsp) salt, and add the cabbage. Cook for 2 minutes. Drain, rinse in cold water and then drain again. Season the cabbage with 5ml (1 tsp) of the sugar and 15ml (1 tbsp) of the cooked oil. Mix well and keep on one side. Place the pork in a dish and mix with the dark soy sauce. Leave for 10 minutes. Drain. Mix all the seasoning ingredients together.

Facing page: Steamed Pork with Salted Cabbage (top), Pork with Green Pepper (page 84) (centre right) and Pork Chop Suey (page 88) (bottom). This page: Spiced Beef (top), Steamed Beef Szechuan Style (bottom left) and Beef with Green Pepper and Chilli (bottom right).

Heat the oil for deep frying and fry the pork until it turns lightly golden. Drain and add to the seasoning mixture. Keep the oil for future use. Place the pork and the seasoning mixture into a deep dish and put the boiled cabbage on top. Cover and steam over boiling water for 1 hour. Drain off any excess liquid and retain. Heat the wok and add the cabbage liquid. Add the blended sauce thickening of cornflour and water. Stir over the heat until the sauce thickens. Pour over the cabbage and pork and serve.

Spiced Beef

PREPARATION TIME: 30 minutes

COOKING TIME: 5-6 minutes

SERVES: 4 people

MARINADE
5ml (1 tsp) sugar
2-3 star anise, ground
2.5ml (½ tsp) ground fennel
15ml (1 tbsp) dark soy sauce
1.25ml (¼ tsp) monosodium glutamate (optional)

450g (1lb) fillet of beef, cut into 2.5cm (1-inch) strips
2.5cm (1-inch) fresh root ginger, peeled and crushed
2.5ml (½ tsp) salt
30ml (2 tbsps) oil
4 spring onions, sliced
2.5ml (½ tsp) freshly ground black pepper
15ml (1 tbsp) light soy sauce

Mix the marinade ingredients together. Add the beef strips, ginger and salt, and marinate for 20 minutes. Heat the oil in wok and stir-fry the onions for 1 minute. Add beef, ground pepper and soy sauce and stir-fry for 4-5 minutes. Serve with a dip.

Beef with Green Pepper and Chilli

PREPARATION TIME: 30 minutes

COOKING TIME: 10-12 minutes

SERVES: 4 people

450g (1lb) fillet of beef, cut into 2.5cm (1-inch) strips

SEASONING
30ml (2 tbsps) dark soy sauce
5ml (1 tsp) sesame oil
Pinch bicarbonate of soda

1.25ml (¼ tsp) ground black pepper
2.5ml (½ tsp) salt
Oil for cooking
2 green peppers, seeded and thinly sliced
1 onion, peeled and sliced
2 spring onions, chopped
2.5cm (1 inch) fresh root ginger, peeled and sliced
2 garlic cloves, peeled and chopped
3 green chillies, sliced

SAUCE
30ml (2 tbsps) chicken stock
2.5ml (½ tsp) monosodium glutamate (optional)
5ml (1 tsp) dark soy sauce
Salt to taste
Few drops sesame oil

Marinate beef with the seasoning ingredients for 15 minutes. Heat 30ml (2 tbsps) oil and stir-fry green peppers and onions for 2 minutes. Remove to a plate. Reheat wok, add 30-45ml (2-3 tbsps) oil and fry ginger, garlic and green chillies for 1 minute. Add beef and stir-fry for 4-5 minutes. Add sauce ingredients, mixed together, and the fried peppers and onions. Stir-fry for a further 2 minutes and serve.

Pork Chow Mein

PREPARATION TIME: 20 minutes
COOKING TIME: 20 minutes
SERVES: 4 people

300g (10oz) egg noodles
450g (1lb) pork, thinly sliced
15ml (1 tbsp) Chinese wine, or dry sherry
5ml (1 tsp) grated root ginger
1 leek, sliced
1 red pepper, cored, seeds removed, and cut into strips
1 stick celery, sliced diagonally
30g (1oz) peas
150ml (¼ pint) chicken or light stock
15ml (1 tbsp) light soy sauce
5ml (1 tsp) sugar
5ml (1 tsp) cornflour
15ml (1 tbsp) water
1 small can bamboo shoots, sliced
45ml (3 tbsps) oil
Salt
Pepper

Soak noodles in hot water for 8 minutes, or as directed. Rinse in cold water, and drain. Combine wine, soy sauce and sugar, and pour over pork. Toss together and set aside for at least 15 minutes. Heat wok and add oil. Add ginger, celery and leek, and stir-fry for 2 minutes. Add red pepper and bamboo shoots, and stir-fry for a further 2 minutes. Remove from wok. Increase heat and add pork, reserving marinade. Stir-fry over high heat for 4 minutes. Return vegetables to wok. Add chicken stock gradually and stir well. Add peas and cook for 2 minutes. Blend cornflour with water. Mix into marinade sauce and stir well. Add noodles and sauce to wok and toss together, heating through as sauce thickens. Add salt and pepper to taste. Simmer for 3 minutes. Serve hot.

Pork with Green Pepper

PREPARATION TIME: 20 minutes
COOKING TIME: 1 hour 15 minutes
SERVES: 4 people

450g (1lb) pork fillet, cut into 5cm (2-inch) strips

SEASONING
1.25ml (¼ tsp) sugar
1.25ml (¼ tsp) monosodium glutamate (optional)
5ml (1 tsp) light soy sauce
10ml (2 tsps) sweet bean paste
10ml (2 tsps) Shao Hsing wine or dry sherry
60ml (4 tbsps) chicken stock

Oil for deep frying
2 cloves garlic, peeled and cut into thin strips
1 green pepper, seeded and sliced into strips
1 green chilli, sliced into strips
1 red chilli, cut in half then sliced into strips

SAUCE
5ml (1 tsp) cornflour
15ml (1 tbsp) water

Boil the pork in water for ¾ hour, until cooked. Drain the pork and discard the water. Mix the seasoning ingredients together and stir in the pork. Leave to stand for 10 minutes. Heat the wok and

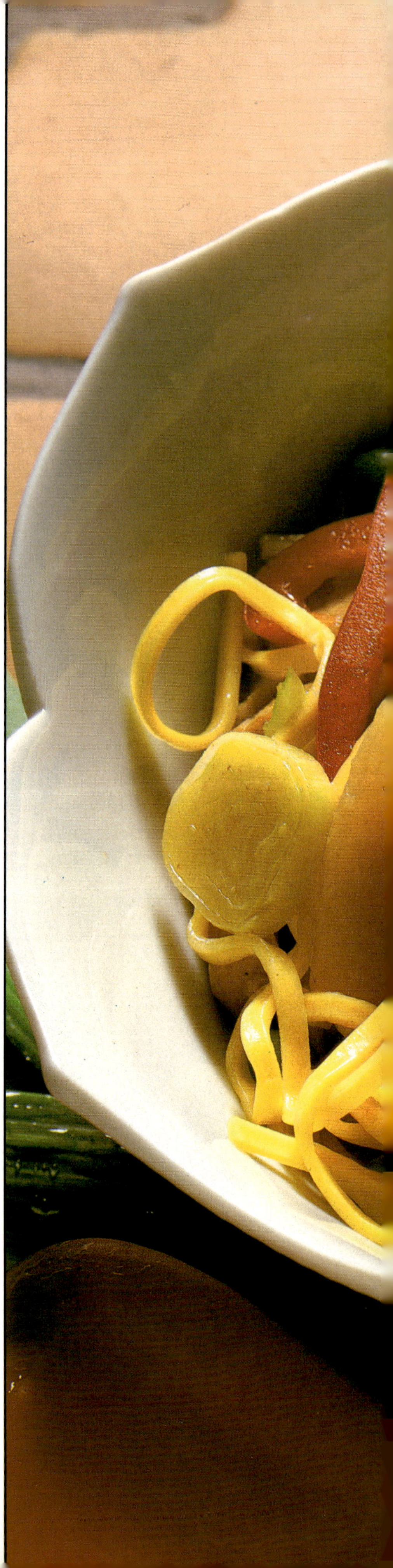

Right: Pork Chow Mein.

add the oil for deep frying. When oil is very hot, fry the drained pork for a few minutes until golden brown. Remove and drain the pork and keep the oil for future use. Reheat the wok, add 5ml (1 tsp) oil, and stir-fry the garlic for 1 minute. Add the pepper and chillies, and stir-fry for 1 minute. Add the remaining seasoning mixture and the pork. Stir-fry over a gentle heat for 1-2 minutes, and then add the blended sauce ingredients. Cook until the sauce thickens. Remove from the heat and serve immediately. Serve with mixed fried rice or rice noodles.

Pork with Plum Sauce

PREPARATION TIME: 40 minutes

COOKING TIME: 30 minutes

SERVES: 4 people

450g (1lb) lean pork fillet, cut into 2.5cm (1-inch) cubes
15ml (1 tbsp) cornflour
5ml (1 tsp) sesame oil
15ml (1 tbsp) light soy sauce
15ml (1 tbsp) sherry
15ml (1 tbsp) brown sugar
2.5ml (½) tsp cinnamon
1 clove garlic, crushed
1 spring onion, sliced finely
30ml (2 tbsps) peanut oil
60ml (4 tbsps) bottled plum sauce
60ml (4 tbsps) water
Salt
Pepper

GARNISH
Spring onion flowers

Mix together the cornflour, sesame oil, light soy sauce, sherry, brown sugar, cinnamon and salt. Pour over pork, and toss together. Leave to marinate for at least 30 minutes. Remove pork and reserve marinade. Heat wok and add peanut oil. Add pork, and stir-fry until golden brown all over. Add spring onion, plum sauce and water to wok, and mix together well. Bring to boil, cover, and simmer gently for 15 minutes, or until pork is tender, stirring occasionally. Add marinade, and bring to boil. Simmer gently for a further 5 minutes. Garnish with spring onion flowers. (To make these, cut spring onion into 5cm (2-inch) lengths.

This page: Pork with Plum Sauce. Facing page: Beef with Green Beans (page 98) (top), Beef Steak with Ginger (page 88) (centre right) and Sweet and Sour Beef (page 103) (bottom).

Carefully cut lengths into fine shreds, keeping one end intact, and then soak in cold water until curling.) Serve hot with boiled rice.

Pork Chop Suey

PREPARATION TIME: 35 minutes

COOKING TIME: 10 minutes

SERVES: 3-4 people

MARINADE
15ml (1 tbsp) water
2.5ml (½ tsp) bicarbonate of soda
10ml (2 tsps) dark soy sauce

225g (½lb) pork fillet, sliced into 5cm (2-inch) pieces
45ml (3 tbsps) cooked oil or cooking oil
1 onion, peeled and cut into pieces
1 clove of garlic, peeled and sliced
25g (1oz) bamboo shoots, sliced
175g (6oz) bean sprouts

SEASONING
Pinch salt
Pinch freshly ground black pepper
Pinch monosodium glutamate (optional)
45ml (3 tbsps) light soy sauce
5ml (1 tsp) sugar
5ml (1 tsp) cornflour

SAUCE
5ml (1 tsp) cornflour
15ml (1 tbsp) water

Mix the marinade ingredients together. Add the pork and leave for 15 minutes to marinate. Drain the pork and discard the marinade. Heat the oil in the wok and stir-fry pork for 2-3 minutes. Remove the pork. Add the onions, garlic and bamboo shoots to the wok and stir-fry for 1-2 minutes. Add the bean sprouts and stir-fry for 2 minutes. Remove to a dish and add the mixed seasoning ingredients. Leave for 10 minutes. Return the pork and the vegetables to the wok. Add the blended sauce ingredients. Bring gently to the boil, stirring until the sauce thickens. Serve immediately.

Lamb Meatballs with Yogurt

PREPARATION TIME: 15 minutes

COOKING TIME: 30 minutes

SERVES: 4 people

450g (1lb)lean minced lamb
2 cloves garlic, crushed
1 small onion, peeled and grated
2.5ml (½ tsp) chilli powder
5ml (1 tsp) garam masala
15ml (1 tbsp) chopped mint
30g (1oz) breadcrumbs
1 egg, lightly beaten
30ml (2 tbsps) oil
75ml (5 tbsps) plain yogurt
Small pinch of saffron strands, or ¼ tsp ground turmeric
30ml (2 tbsps) boiling water
Salt
Pepper

GARNISH
Fresh coriander or mint

In a bowl, mix together minced lamb, garlic, onion, chilli powder, garam masala, mint and breadcrumbs. Add lightly beaten egg to bind ingredients together. Add salt and pepper to taste. Wet hands. Take a teaspoon of mixture, and roll between palms, forming small balls. Heat wok and add oil. Add meatballs, shake wok to make meatballs roll around, and fry until well browned all over. Add saffron or turmeric to 30ml (2 tbsps) boiling water. Leave for 5 minutes. Add water to yogurt, and stir until evenly mixed. Reheat meatballs and serve on yogurt. Garnish with mint or fresh coriander. Serve with rice.

Pork with Black Bean Sauce

PREPARATION TIME: 40 minutes

COOKING TIME: 45 minutes

SERVES: 4 people

225g (8oz) lean pork, cut into 2.5cm (1-inch) cubes
15ml (1 tbsp) oil
1 red pepper, cored, seeds removed, and sliced

SAUCE
45ml (3 tbsps) black beans, rinsed in cold water and crushed with back of a spoon
30ml (2 tbsps) Chinese wine, or dry sherry
5ml (1 tsp) grated ginger
30ml (2 tbsps) light soy sauce
3 cloves garlic, crushed
15ml (1 tbsp) cornflour
150ml (¼ pint) water

Mix together black beans, wine, ginger, soy sauce and garlic. Blend cornflour with 30ml (2 tbsps) water and add to bean mixture. Place pork in a bowl, and pour over sauce. Toss together well. Leave for at least 30 minutes. Heat wok, add oil and stir-fry red pepper for 3 minutes. Remove and set aside. Add pork, reserving marinade sauce. Stir-fry pork until well browned all over. Add marinade sauce and remaining water. Bring to the boil. Reduce heat, cover, and simmer gently for about 30 minutes, until pork is tender, stirring occasionally. Add more water if necessary. Just before serving, add red pepper and heat through. Serve with plain white rice.

Beef Steak with Ginger

PREPARATION TIME: 20-25 minutes

COOKING TIME: 10-12 minutes

SERVES: 2-3 people

SEASONING
2.5ml (½ tsp) bicarbonate of soda
45ml (3 tbsps) light soy sauce
30ml (2 tbsps) rice wine or dry sherry
2.5ml (½ tsp) salt
2.5ml (½ tsp) ground black pepper
1.25cm (½ tsp) fresh root ginger, peeled and minced

225g (½lb) beef fillet, sliced into 2.5cm (1-inch) pieces

SAUCE
5ml (1 tsp) sugar
1.25ml (¼ tsp) monosodium glutamate (optional)
15ml (1 tbsp) dark soy sauce
45ml (3 tbsps) stock

Facing page: Lamb Meatballs with Yogurt (top) and Pork with Black Bean Sauce (bottom).

Few drops sesame oil
5ml (1 tsp) Shao Hsing wine

60ml (4 tbsps) oil
2.5cm (1 inch) fresh root ginger, peeled and thinly sliced
4 spring onions, chopped
50g (2oz) bamboo shoots, thinly sliced
2 green chillies, sliced

Mix together the seasoning ingredients, add the beef and marinate for 20 minutes. Drain the beef and discard the marinade. Mix the sauce ingredients together. Heat 45ml (3 tbsps) oil in the wok and fry the sliced ginger and onions for 2 minutes. Add the bamboo shoots and chillies and stir-fry for 1-2 minutes. Remove to a plate. Add the remaining oil to the wok and fry the beef for 2-3 minutes. Add fried vegetables and stir-fry for 2 minutes. Add well-stirred sauce ingredients and simmer gently until the mixture thickens. Simmer for another 1-2 minutes. Remove from heat and serve.

Sweet and Sour Pork with Peppers

PREPARATION TIME: 1 hour 15 minutes

COOKING TIME: 30 minutes

SERVES: 4 people

450g (1lb) pork fillets, cut into 2.5cm (1-inch cubes)
1 large green pepper, cored, seeds removed, and chopped roughly
1 large yellow or red pepper, cored, seeds removed, and chopped roughly
1 small can or jar of Chinese mixed pickle
1 large onion, peeled and chopped finely
300ml (½ pint) peanut oil

BATTER
1 egg
5ml (1 tsp) peanut oil
60ml (4 tbsps) cornflour
60ml (4 tbsps) self-raising flour
Water

MARINADE
15ml (1 tbsp) peanut oil
2.5ml (½ tsp) light soy sauce
10ml (2 tsps) Chinese wine, or 15ml (1 tbsp) dry sherry
5ml (1 tsp) cornflour
5ml (1 tsp) sugar
Pinch of salt
Pinch of pepper

SAUCE
60ml (4 tbsps) sugar
100ml (3½ fl oz) wine vinegar
100ml (3½ fl oz) water
15ml (1 tbsp) tomato purée
Pinch of salt
5ml (1 tsp) cornflour
Pinch of red food colouring (if desired)

Mix together marinade ingredients. Pour over pork pieces and leave for about 1 hour, turning occasionally. Mix together batter ingredients with enough water to form batter. Add pork. Heat peanut oil in wok. When hot, deep-fry pork pieces in small batches, so that they do not stick together. Remove when golden brown, using a slotted spoon, and set aside. Continue until all battered pork pieces are cooked. Heat oil again and repeat process, cooking pork for 5 minutes to make batter nice and crisp. Keep warm. Carefully drain off all but 15ml (1 tbsp) of oil. Heat, and add onion, peppers and Chinese mixed pickle. Cover and cook for 3 minutes. Remove and set aside. Heat vinegar, water, sugar, tomato purée, red food colouring and salt. Slake cornflour with 15ml (1 tbsp) of water. Stir into sauce. Bring to the boil and cook for 3 minutes. Add pork and vegetables to sauce. Serve hot with rice.

Beef Worcestershire

PREPARATION TIME: 40 minutes

COOKING TIME: 20 minutes

SERVES: 4 people

450g (1lb) fillet or rump steak, cut into 4cm (1½-inch) cubes
60g (2oz) wonton wrappers
150ml (¼ pint) oil for deep frying

Beef Worcestershire (top right) and Sweet and Sour Pork with Peppers (bottom right).

SAUCE
30ml (2 tbsps) Worcestershire sauce
15ml (1 tbsp) dark soy sauce
15ml (1 tbsp) sugar
Pinch of salt
Pinch of pepper
2.5ml (½ tsp) cornflour

Mix together ingredients for sauce, and pour over steak. Toss well. Leave for at least 30 minutes, turning occasionally. Meanwhile, heat oil in wok. Fold wonton wrappers in half diagonally, seal open corners with water and press together. Deep-fry a few wonton wrappers at a time until golden brown. Remove with a slotted spoon and drain on absorbent paper. Repeat until there are enough wonton wrappers to go around the edge of the serving dish. Carefully remove all but 30ml (2 tbsps) of oil from wok. Remove steak from sauce mixture and reserve. Heat wok and, when oil is hot, add steak and stir-fry until well browned. Pour over sauce and bring to the boil. Reduce heat and simmer, stirring continuously. When sauce thickens and will coat steak well, place in warm serving dish and garnish with wonton wrappers. Serve immediately with boiled rice.

Beef with Green Pepper, Tomato and Black Beans

PREPARATION TIME: 30 minutes

MICROWAVE COOKING TIME: 8-10 minutes

SERVES: 4 people

450g (1lb) rump steak, cut in thin slices
60ml (4 tbsps) soy sauce
10ml (2 tbsps) dry sherry or rice wine

SAUCE
45ml (3 tbsps) salted black beans
30ml (2 tbsps) water
280ml (8 fl oz) brown stock
15ml (1 tbsp) sugar
30ml (3 tbsps) cornflour dissolved in the stock
1 clove garlic, finely minced
1 large green pepper, cut in 2.5cm (1-inch) pieces
3 tomatoes, peeled and quartered
Salt and pepper

This page: Beef with Green Pepper, Tomato and Black Beans. Facing page: Pork Chops, Shanghai Style (top) and Lion's Head (page 94) (bottom).

Mix together the steak, soy sauce and wine and leave to marinate, covered, in the refrigerator for 30 minutes. Crush the black beans and mix with the water. Leave to stand until ready to use. Combine all the ingredients in a shallow dish, except for the pepper and tomatoes. Cover the dish and cook on HIGH for 7-9 minutes, stirring halfway through the cooking time. Once the sauce has cleared, add the pepper and tomatoes and cook 1 minute further on HIGH. Serve with rice. Garnish with spring onion brushes if desired.

Pork Chops, Shanghai Style

PREPARATION TIME: 15 minutes

MICROWAVE COOKING TIME: 14 minutes

SERVES: 4 people

90ml (3 fl oz) soy sauce
15ml (1 tbsp) brown sugar
15ml (1 tbsp) oil
8 thin pork chops

1 onion, thinly sliced
10ml (2 tsps) cornflour mixed with 10ml (2 tsps) water

Mix the soy sauce and sugar with 120ml (4 fl oz) water. Heat a browning dish 5 minutes on HIGH. Pour in the oil and brown the pork on both sides about 2 minutes on HIGH. Brown in two batches if necessary. Remove the pork and add the onion. Cook to brown and soften slightly. Remove the onion from the browning dish and set aside. Return the pork chops to the dish and pour over the soy sauce mixture. Cover and cook a further 5 minutes on HIGH, or until the pork is tender. Remove the pork and keep warm. Mix the cornflour and water with the soy sauce mixture. Stir well and cook 1 minute on HIGH to thicken slightly. Add the onions and cook a further 1 minute on HIGH. Pour over the pork to serve. Serve with stir-fried vegetables. Garnish with Chinese parsley leaves if desired.

Pork with Chilli

PREPARATION TIME: 1 hour

COOKING TIME: 20 minutes

SERVES: 4 people

300g (10oz) lean pork fillet, cut into 2.5cm (1-inch) cubes
1 green pepper, cored, seeds removed, and sliced
1 red chilli, seeds removed, and sliced finely
4 spring onions, chopped
1 clove garlic, crushed
5ml (1 tsp) sugar
5ml (1 tsp) cornflour
5ml (1 tsp) peanut oil
5ml (1 tsp) Chinese wine or dry sherry
150ml (¼ pint) peanut oil, for deep frying

SAUCE
5ml (1 tsp) chilli powder
30ml (2 tbsps) dark soy sauce
5ml (1 tsp) Worcestershire sauce
2.5ml (½ tsp) five-spice powder
Pinch of salt

Mix together garlic, sugar, 5ml (1 tsp) peanut oil, wine and cornflour, and pour over pork. Cover and leave for at least 1 hour, turning occasionally. Meanwhile, combine sauce ingredients in a bowl. Mix well and set aside. Heat oil in wok until hot. Toss in pork cubes, and cook until golden brown and cooked through – about 10 minutes. Drain and set aside. Carefully remove all but 15ml (1 tbsp) of oil from wok. Heat oil and add green pepper, chilli and spring onions. Stir-fry for 2 minutes. Add sauce and pork, and bring to the boil, stirring continuously. Adjust seasoning. Serve immediately with rice or noodles.

Happy's Curry

PREPARATION TIME: 20 minutes

COOKING TIME: 30 minutes

SERVES: 4 people

450g (1lb) skirt or rump steak, cut into 2.5cm (1-inch) cubes
225g (8oz) potatoes, peeled and diced
2 onions, peeled and chopped very finely
3 cloves garlic, crushed
5ml (1 tsp) grated root ginger
5ml (1 tsp) ground turmeric
2.5ml (½) tsp chilli powder
5ml (1 tsp) garam masala
2.5ml (½) tsp salt
300ml (½ pint) water
60ml (4 tbsps) peanut oil

GARNISH
Fresh coriander

Heat wok and add oil. Add ginger, garlic and onions, and fry gently for 5 minutes. Add turmeric, chilli powder, garam masala and salt, and fry for 30 seconds. Add steak and stir-fry until browned well all over. Add potatoes and water, and bring to the boil. Reduce heat, and cover. Simmer gently until meat is tender and potatoes are cooked. Garnish with fresh coriander and serve with rice, if desired.

Lion's Head

PREPARATION TIME: 20 minutes

MICROWAVE COOKING TIME: 19-20 minutes

SERVES: 4-6 people

900g (2lbs) minced pork
90ml (3 fl oz) soy sauce
10ml (2 tsps) dry sherry
5ml (1 tsp) brown sugar
60g (2oz) cornflour
30ml (2 tbsps) oil
5ml (1 tsp) granulated sugar
25ml (1½ tbsps) soy sauce

Pork with Chilli (right) and Happy's Curry (below).

1 head Chinese leaves
Salt (if necessary)

Mix pork, 90ml (3 fl oz) soy sauce, sherry, brown sugar and 15ml (1 tbsp) cornflour, and shape into 5cm (2-inch) balls. Heat a browning dish 5 minutes on HIGH. Add the oil and the pork balls. Brown the pork balls 3-5 minutes on HIGH, turning often. Cook in 2 batches, re-heating the dish in between each batch. If the browning dish has a cover, leave the pork balls in it or transfer to a large casserole. Add the granulated sugar, 25ml (1½) tbsps soy sauce and 280ml (½ pint) water. Cover and cook 9 minutes on HIGH. Turn the pork balls often and rearrange to bring those in the middle of the dish to the outside. Shred the Chinese leaves finely and add to the casserole with the pork balls. Cook 1 minute on HIGH. Remove the pork and Chinese leaves to a serving dish and keep warm. Mix the remaining cornflour with 30ml (2 tbsps) water and add to the cooking liquid from the pork balls. Cook 2-3 minutes, uncovered, on HIGH or until the sauce has thickened. Arrange the cabbage on a serving dish with the pork balls on top. Pour over the sauce to serve.

Kung-Pao Lamb

PREPARATION TIME: 20 minutes

MICROWAVE COOKING TIME: 10½-11½ minutes

SERVES: 4 people

450g (1lb) lamb fillet or meat from the leg, thinly sliced
30ml (2 tbsps) oil
1 clove garlic, finely minced
1 small piece fresh ginger root, grated
½ red chilli pepper, finely chopped
60ml (4 tbsps) soy sauce
120ml (4 fl oz) stock
30ml (2 tbsps) white wine
5ml (1 tsp) vinegar
5ml (1 tsp) sugar
15ml (1 tbsp) cornflour
1 small red pepper, cut in small dice
1 small green pepper, cut in small dice
4 spring onions, sliced
60g (2oz) roasted peanuts
Dash sesame oil

Heat a browning dish for 5 minutes on HIGH. Combine oil and lamb and add to the dish. Cook for about 2 minutes, turning often. Cook in two batches if necessary. Add the garlic, ginger and chilli pepper and cook a further 2 minutes on HIGH. Mix the soy sauce, stock, wine, vinegar, sugar and cornflour together and add to the meat. Cover the browning dish or transfer the ingredients to a covered casserole dish. Cook on MEDIUM a further 4-6 minutes, or until the lamb is tender. Add the diced peppers and cook a further 1 minute on HIGH. Stir in the sesame oil, peanuts and the spring onions. Heat 30 seconds on HIGH. Serve with rice.

Shredded Pork with Preserved Vegetables

PREPARATION TIME: 30 minutes

COOKING TIME: 6-8 minutes

SERVES: 3-4 people

Pinch monosodium glutamate (optional)
10ml (2 tsps) cornflour
Salt and freshly ground black pepper to taste
225g (½lb) lean pork, shredded
Oil
2.5cm (1 inch) fresh root ginger, peeled and shredded
50g (2oz) shelled green peas
2.5ml (½ tsp) sugar
10ml (2 tsps) Shao Hsing wine or dry sherry
225g (8oz) Shanghai preserved vegetables (mixed) in brine
5ml (1 tsp) sesame oil

Facing page: Kung Pao Lamb. This page: Sweet and Sour Pork (top), Diced Pork with Walnuts (page 108) (centre) and Shredded Pork with Preserved Vegetables (bottom).

Mix together the monosodium glutamate, cornflour and a pinch of salt. Add the pork and let it stand for 15 minutes. Heat the oil in a wok and deep-fry the pork for 3 minutes. Remove the pork and drain. Reserve oil for future use. Reheat wok and add 10ml (2 tsps) deep-fried oil. Stir-fry the ginger and green peas for 1 minute. Add the pork and sprinkle with the sugar, wine and salt and pepper to taste. Stir-fry for another minute and add the well-drained, preserved vegetables. Allow to heat through and then stir gently. Sprinkle on the sesame oil and serve. Serve as a side dish or on a bed of plain fried noodles.

Sweet and Sour Pork

PREPARATION TIME: 20 minutes, plus 20 minutes to marinate

COOKING TIME: 15-20 minutes

SERVES: 4 people

BATTER
45ml (3 tbsps) flour
15ml (1 tbsp) cornflour
7.5ml (1½ tsps) bicarbonate of soda
30ml (2 tbsps) oil

350g (12oz) lean pork, cut into 2.5cm (1-inch) cubes

SEASONING
5ml (1 tsp) sugar
5ml (1 tsp) salt
30ml (2 tbsps) light soy sauce
5ml (1 tsp) dark soy sauce
15ml (1 tbsp) cooked oil
15ml (1 tbsp) water

Cornflour
Oil for deep frying
2 cloves garlic, cut into thin strips
1 large onion, peeled and cut into 1cm (½-inch) pieces
1 carrot, sliced into 3x25x50mm (⅛x1x2-inch) thin pieces
Pinch salt

SWEET AND SOUR SAUCE
45ml (3 tbsps) sugar
15ml (1 tbsp) tomato purée
250ml (8 fl oz) chicken stock or water
60ml (4 tbsps) red or white vinegar
5ml (1 tsp) light soy sauce
Few slices fresh root ginger, peeled
15ml (1 tbsp) cornflour
Few drops of red food colouring
10ml (2 tsps) cooked oil

Mix the batter ingredients together, adding sufficient water to make a thick coating batter. Wash and drain the pork. Mix with the seasoning ingredients and marinate for 15-20 minutes. Drain the pork and discard the marinade. Roll the pork cubes in cornflour. Heat the oil for deep frying. Dip the pork cubes in batter and fry in the hot oil until golden brown. Fry a few at a time until all the pork has been fried. Drain well and keep warm in a low oven. Heat wok and add 10ml (2 tsps) deep-fried oil. Stir-fry the garlic, onions and carrots for 3-4 minutes. Season with salt and fry for a further minute. Mix the sweet and sour sauce ingredients together and add to the wok. Stir the mixture until it thickens. Pour over the fried pork cubes and serve immediately. Note: sliced green peppers can also be added along with the carrots and onions.

Beef with Green Beans

PREPARATION TIME: 30 minutes

COOKING TIME: 12 minutes

SERVES: 4 people

SEASONING

2.5ml (½ tsp) bicarbonate of soda
5ml (1 tsp) cornflour
15ml (1 tbsp) light soy sauce
30ml (2 tbsps) water
5ml (1 tsp) cooked oil
450g (1lb) lean beef, thinly sliced into 2.5cm (1-inch) pieces

SAUCE

1.25ml (¼ tsp) salt
5ml (1 tsp) monosodium glutamate (optional)
5ml (1 tsp) light soy sauce
5ml (1 tsp) dark soy sauce
5ml (1 tsp) Shao Hsing wine (optional)
120ml (4 fl oz) stock
10ml (2 tsps) cornflour
45ml (3 tbsps) oil
2 cloves of garlic, peeled and sliced
1 onion, peeled and cut into wedges
2.5cm (1 inch) fresh ginger root, peeled and sliced thinly
175g (6oz) Chinese long beans, cut into 7.5cm (3-inch) pieces, or whole tender green beans
Salt and freshly ground black pepper to taste

Mix seasoning ingredients together. Add the beef and marinate for 20 minutes. Drain the meat and discard the marinade. Mix the sauce ingredients together. Heat 30ml (2 tbsps) oil in the wok until it smokes. Reduce the heat, add the garlic and the beef, and stir-fry for 3-4 minutes. Remove the meat and keep on one side. Heat the remaining oil in the wok, add the onion, ginger and long beans and stir-fry for 2-3 minutes. Add fried beef. Cover and fry for a further 1 minute. Stir in the sauce ingredients and bring to the boil. Simmer gently for 2-3 minutes. Season with salt and pepper. Remove from heat and serve.

Spiced Liver

PREPARATION TIME: 10 minutes

COOKING TIME: 20 minutes

SERVES: 4 people

450g (1lb) lamb's liver, cut into 2.5cm (1-inch) cubes
120ml (4 fl oz) soy sauce
3-4 spring onions, chopped
30ml (2 tbsps) rice wine or dry sherry
10ml (2 tsps) sugar
2.5cm (1 inch) fresh root ginger, peeled and finely chopped
2.5cm (½ tsp) freshly ground black pepper
Pinch anise powder

Boil the liver for 3-4 minutes in sufficient water just to cover. Drain well. Add soy sauce, spring onions, wine, sugar, ginger, pepper and anise powder. Simmer gently for 10-15 minutes, covered, until the liver is tender. Serve as a side dish.

Braised Hong Kong Beef

PREPARATION TIME: 30 minutes

COOKING TIME: about 15-17 minutes

SERVES: 4 people

30ml (2 tbsps) oil
450g (1lb) fillet of beef, sliced into matchstick-size strips
1 onion, peeled and sliced
2.5cm (1 inch) fresh root ginger, peeled and cut into thin strips
3-4 fresh tomatoes, cut into thin wedges
225g (½lb) carrots, scraped and cut into 5cm (2-inch) sticks
10ml (2 tsps) brown sugar
2.5ml (½ tsp) five-spice powder
30ml (2 tbsps) light soy sauce
15ml (1 tbsp) rice wine or dry sherry
30ml (2 tbsps) water
Salt to taste

Spiced Liver (top) and Braised Hong Kong Beef (right).

Heat the oil in a wok and fry the beef for 3-4 minutes. Add the onion, ginger, tomatoes and carrots. Stir-fry for 2-3 minutes. Add the sugar, five-spice powder, soy sauce, wine and water. Season with salt to taste and cook gently for 8-10 minutes. Serve as a side dish.

Devilled Kidneys

PREPARATION TIME: 1 hour 15 minutes

COOKING TIME: 20 minutes

SERVES: 4 people

450g (1lb) veal kidneys
15ml (1 tbsp) Worcestershire sauce
15ml (1 tbsp) dark soy sauce
30g (1oz) butter
5ml (1 tsp) cornflour
15ml (1 tbsp) water

DEVILLING MIXTURE
5ml (1 tsp) salt
5ml (1 tsp) sugar
2.5ml (½ tsp) ground black pepper
2.5ml (½ tsp) ground ginger
2.5ml (½ tsp) dry mustard
1.25ml (¼ tsp) curry powder

GARNISH
Sprig of parsley

Skin the kidneys and cut in half lengthways. Mix the dry devilling mixture together, and coat kidneys well. Leave for at least 1 hour. Heat wok and melt butter. Brown the kidneys quickly in the hot butter. Add Worcestershire sauce and soy sauce, and bring to the boil. Cover and simmer for 15 minutes, thickening with cornflour mixed with water if necessary. Garnish with parsley and serve with rice.

Calves' Liver with Piquant Sauce

PREPARATION TIME: 10 minutes

COOKING TIME: 25 minutes

SERVES: 4 people

450g (1lb) calves' liver
1 onion, peeled and sliced
15ml (1 tbsp) oil
30g (1oz) butter
15ml (1 tbsp) flour
300ml (½ pint) brown stock, or 300ml (½ pint) hot water and 1 beef stock cube
30ml (2 tbsps) tomato, mango, or other fruit chutney
15ml (1 tbsp) tomato purée
1 clove garlic, crushed
5ml (1 tsp) made mustard, English style
Salt
Pepper

This page: Devilled Kidneys (top) and Calves' Liver with Piquant Sauce (bottom). Facing page: Kidneys with Bacon (page 106) (top) and Piquant Lambs' Livers (page 108) (bottom).

GARNISH
Chopped parsley

Heat wok and add butter. When melted, stir in flour and cook until lightly browned. Remove from heat and gradually stir in stock. Return to heat and add tomato purée and garlic. Stir until boiling. Add mustard and salt and pepper to taste, and let simmer for 5 minutes. Add chutney and mix well. Remove from wok and set aside. Meanwhile, slice liver very thinly. Wash and drain on absorbent paper. Heat wok and add oil. When hot add onion. Fry gently over medium heat until just turning colour. Add slices of liver in a single layer, and fry for about 3 minutes on each side, depending on thickness of slices. The liver should be cooked through and still tender. Do not overcook. Add piquant sauce to wok and toss together. Sprinkle with chopped parsley. Serve immediately on boiled rice.

Steamed Lamb with Mushroom Sauce

PREPARATION TIME: 20-25 minutes
COOKING TIME: 2 hours 10 minutes
SERVES: 6 people

1kg (2¼lb) boned leg of lamb, cut into 2.5cm (1-inch) cubes
2 onions, thinly sliced
Salt and freshly ground black pepper
10ml (2 tsps) oil
2 cloves of garlic, peeled and sliced
5ml (1 tsp) cornflour
Pinch monosodium glutamate (optional)
75ml (5 tbsps) light soy sauce
45ml (3 tbsps) rice wine or dry sherry
5ml (1 tsp) crushed black pepper
2.5cm (1 inch) fresh root ginger, peeled and thinly sliced
Few drops sesame oil

Put the lamb into a saucepan and add sufficient water to cover. Boil for 5 minutes. Drain the lamb and retain the water. Arrange the lamb cubes in a deep dish and sprinkle the onions on top. Season with salt and pepper. Heat the oil in a wok and fry the garlic until brown. Remove the garlic and discard. Mix together the cornflour, monosodium glutamate, soy sauce, wine, crushed pepper, ginger and 60ml (4 tbsps) reserved water. Stir the cornflour mixture into the oil in the wok and cook for 1-2 minutes. Pour over the lamb. Cover the lamb with overlapping foil and tie around the rim. Put the dish in a steamer and steam over boiling water for 2 hours. Serve with the sesame oil sprinkled over the lamb.

Lamb with Tomatoes

PREPARATION TIME: 20 minutes
COOKING TIME: about 10 minutes
SERVES: 2 people

10ml (2 tsps) cornflour
2.5ml (½ tsp) salt
15ml (1 tbsp) light soy sauce
60ml (4 tbsps) water
45ml (3 tbsps) oil
1cm (½ inch) fresh root ginger, sliced
225g (½lb) lamb fillet, cut across the grain in thin strips of 1x5cm (½x2 inches)
2 spring onions, chopped
1 onion, peeled and cut into 2.5cm (1-inch) pieces
1 green pepper, seeded and cut into strips
5ml (1 tsp) curry powder
3-4 small, firm tomatoes, cut into 1cm (½-inch) pieces

Mix together the cornflour, salt, soy sauce, water and 5ml (1 tsp) of the oil. Keep on one side. Heat the remaining oil in a wok and fry the ginger and lamb for 2-3 minutes. Add the onions, green pepper and curry powder and stir-fry for 3-4 minutes. Stir in the cornflour mixture and cook for 1 minute. Add the tomatoes and cook until the sauce thickens. Serve as a side dish.

Mongolian Lamb with Onions

PREPARATION TIME: 20 minutes
COOKING TIME: 8-10 minutes
SERVES: 4 people

450g (1lb) lean, boned lamb, cut into 5x50mm (¼x2-inch) strips
1 egg white
2 cloves of garlic, sliced
2.5ml (½ tsp) five-spice powder
1cm (½ inch) fresh root ginger, peeled and thinly sliced
15ml (1 tbsp) cornflour
15ml (1 tbsp) light soy sauce
45ml (3 tbsps) rice wine or dry sherry
30ml (2 tbsps) water
45ml (3 tbsps) cooked oil
6 spring onions, chopped

Mix the lamb with the egg white, garlic, five-spice powder, ginger root and 5ml (1 tsp) cornflour and 5ml (1 tsp) soy sauce. Keep on one side. Mix the remaining cornflour, soy sauce, wine and water together. Heat the wok and add the oil. When it begins to smoke, add the beef mixture. Reduce the heat and stir-fry for 3-4 minutes, until the meat browns slightly. Remove and keep on one side. Add the onions and the cornflour, soy sauce and wine mixture to the wok. Stir until it

Sweet and Sour Beef

PREPARATION TIME: 15 minutes

COOKING TIME: 15 minutes

SERVES: 4 people

BATTER

100g (4oz) plain flour
7.5ml (1½ tsps) baking powder
60ml (4 tbsps) cornflour
15ml (1 tbsp) oil

45ml (3 tbsps) oil

225g (8oz) fillet of beef, cut into 2.5cm (1-inch) cubes
1 onion, peeled and cut into wedges
2.5cm (1-inch) fresh root ginger, peeled and thinly sliced
1 clove garlic, peeled and thinly sliced
1 green pepper, seeded and chopped

SWEET AND SOUR SAUCE

60ml (4 tbsps) sugar
1.25ml (¼ tsp) salt
60ml (4 tbsps) red or malt vinegar
5ml (1 tsp) fresh root ginger, peeled and minced
90ml (6 tbsps) water
15ml (1 tbsp) cornflour
10ml (2 tsps) cooked oil
Few drops food colouring
Oil for deep frying

Lamb with Tomatoes (far left), Steamed Lamb with Mushroom Sauce (left) and Mongolian Lamb with Onions (below).

For the batter: sieve the flour, baking powder and cornflour. Beat in the oil and add sufficient water to make a thick, smooth batter. Heat the 45ml (3 tbsps) oil in a wok and stir-fry the beef for 2 minutes. Remove the beef. Fry the onion, ginger, garlic and green pepper for 2-3 minutes in the same oil. Remove the wok from the heat. Mix the sauce ingredients together and add to the wok. Return the wok to the heat and bring to the boil gently. Lower the heat and simmer gently for 2-3 minutes, until thick and clear. Meanwhile, dip the beef cubes into the batter and deep-fry in hot oil until golden brown and crisp. Drain on absorbent paper. Arrange in a deep dish and pour the hot sauce over the beef. Serve with a chow mein dish or fried rice. Thinly sliced carrot, cucumber and courgette may also be added along with the onion, ginger and green pepper.

Steak with Peanut Sauce

PREPARATION TIME: 45 minutes

COOKING TIME: 30 minutes

SERVES: 4 people

450g (1lb) fillet or rump steak, cut into 1.5cm (½-inch) cubes
15ml (1 tbsp) oil

MARINADE
2.5ml (½ tsp) chilli powder
Juice of half a lemon
30ml (2 tsps) brown sugar
2.5ml (½ tsp) salt
5ml (1 tsp) ground coriander
5ml (1 tsp) ground cumin

PEANUT SAUCE
30ml (2 tbsps) peanut oil
60g (2oz) raw shelled peanuts
2 red chillies, seeds removed, and chopped (or 1 tsp chilli powder)
2 shallots, chopped
2 clove garlic, crushed
5ml (1 tsp) brown sugar
Juice of half a lemon
Salt

Mix together marinade ingredients, and marinate steak for at least 30 minutes. Make sauce. Heat wok, add half peanut oil and heat gently. Stir-fry peanuts for 2-3 minutes. Remove from wok, and drain on absorbent paper. Crush chillies, shallots and garlic to a smooth paste, or blend. Grind peanuts to fine powder. Heat remaining oil in wok over a medium heat. Fry chilli paste for 1-2 minutes. Add 175ml (6 fl oz) water. Bring to the boil. Add peanuts, brown sugar, lemon juice and salt to taste. Stir until sauce is thick – approximately 10 minutes. Put in bowl, and keep warm. Heat wok, and add oil. Stir-fry meat until well browned all over. Serve with peanut sauce and boiled rice.

Steak with Black Bean Sauce

PREPARATION TIME: 1 hour 15 minutes

COOKING TIME: 20 minutes

SERVES: 4 people

Facing page: Steak with Peanut Sauce (top) and Noodles with Pork and Shrimp (page 106) (bottom). This page: Braised Pork with Spinach and Mushrooms (top) and Steak with Black Bean Sauce (bottom).

225g (8oz) fillet or rump steak, thinly sliced
1 large onion, peeled and chopped
1 large green pepper, cored, seeds removed, and diced
3 cloves garlic, crushed
5ml (1 tsp) grated root ginger
1 small can sliced bamboo shoots, drained
15ml (1 tbsp) black beans
30ml (2 tbsps) light soy sauce
60ml (4 tbsps) peanut oil
5ml (1 tsp) Chinese wine, or 10ml (2 tsps) dry sherry
15ml (1tbsp) sugar
5ml (1 tsp) cornflour
5ml (1 tsp) sesame oil
Pinch of bicarbonate of soda
Salt
Pepper

Put sliced steak into a bowl, and sprinkle over bicarbonate of soda. Add 15ml (1 tbsp) of light soy sauce, 5ml (1 tsp) of sugar, the wine, sesame oil, salt and pepper, and leave to marinate for at least 1 hour. Heat wok and add 30ml (2 tbsps) peanut oil. When hot, add steak and fry quickly. Remove from heat, and remove steak. Set aside. Add onion, green pepper, bamboo shoots, and a pinch of salt to wok. Cover and cook for 3 minutes. Remove and set aside. Make black bean sauce by crushing black beans and mixing with garlic, ginger, 1 tsp of sugar and 15ml (1 tbsp) of peanut oil. Heat wok, add 15ml (1 tbsp) of oil and pour in black bean mixture. Add steak and vegetables and mix well. Make seasoning sauce by mixing cornflour with remaining 15ml (1 tbsp) of light soy sauce, and adding 5ml (1 tsp) sugar. When well mixed, pour into wok and stir. Bring to the boil and cook for 3 minutes. Serve hot with rice.

Braised Pork with Spinach and Mushrooms

PREPARATION TIME: 20 minutes

COOKING TIME: 30 minutes

SERVES: 4 people

450g (1lb) lean pork fillet, cut into thin strips
225g (8oz) spinach leaves, washed, hard stalks removed, and shredded
4 dried Chinese mushrooms, soaked in hot water for 20 minutes, stems discarded, and caps sliced finely
2.5ml (½ tsp) ground nutmeg
30ml (2 tbsps) water
30ml (2 tbsps) peanut oil
1 onion, peeled and quartered
1 clove garlic, crushed
15ml (1 tbsp) flour
Salt
Pepper

Heat wok, add 5ml (1 tsp) of oil, and roll it around to coat the surface. Put nutmeg and spinach in wok, and cook gently for 5 minutes. Remove from pan. Add remaining oil to wok and fry garlic and onion over gentle heat for 5 minutes. Remove from wok. Meanwhile, add a good pinch of salt and freshly-ground black pepper to the flour and toss in the pork, coating well. Fry pork until each piece is browned all over. Add water and mushrooms, and return onion mixture to wok. Cover and simmer gently for 10 minutes, stirring occasionally. Add spinach and salt and pepper to taste, and cook, uncovered, for 2 minutes. Serve hot with steamed rice.

Noodles with Pork and Shrimp

PREPARATION TIME: 20 minutes

COOKING TIME: 15 minutes

SERVES: 4 people

225g (8oz) fine egg noodles
60ml (4 tbsps) peanut oil
1 onion, peeled and chopped finely
115g (4oz) pork, finely sliced
115g (4oz) prawns or shrimp, shelled and de-veined
2 cloves garlic, crushed
15ml (1 tbsp) light soy sauce
5ml (1 tsp) sambal manis or sambal oelek
¼ cabbage, shredded
1 green chilli, seeds removed, and sliced
2 sticks celery, sliced
Salt
Pepper

GARNISH
Sliced cucumber
Sliced spring onions

Soak noodles in hot water for 8 minutes, or boil until cooked. Rinse in cold water. Drain in a colander. Set aside. Heat wok and add oil. Stir-fry onion, garlic and chilli until onion starts to colour. Add sambal manis or sambal oelek. Add pork, celery, cabbage and salt and pepper, and stir-fry for 3 minutes. Add soy sauce, noodles and prawns, and toss mixture to heat through well. Place in a warm serving dish, surrounded with sliced cucumber and sprinkled with spring onions on top.

Lamb with Cherries

PREPARATION TIME: 15 minutes

COOKING TIME: 1 hour 15 minutes

SERVES: 4 people

450g (1lb) boneless lamb from leg, cut into 2.5cm (1-inch) cubes
60g (2oz) butter
1 onion, peeled and chopped finely
2.5 ml (½ tsp) turmeric
2.5 ml (½ tsp) cinnamon
2.5 ml (½ tsp) ground nutmeg
5ml (1 tsp) brown sugar
1 can black cherries, stones removed
15ml (1 tbsp) lemon juice
15ml (1 tbsp) arrowroot
150ml (¼ pint) water
Salt
Pepper

Heat half butter in wok. Add lamb and fry quickly to brown well all over. Remove from wok and set aside. Add remaining butter and onion and fry for 2 minutes. Add turmeric, cinnamon, nutmeg and brown sugar, and fry for a further 1 minute. Add salt and pepper to taste. Return lamb to wok and add water. Cover and simmer gently for 45 minutes to 1 hour, until lamb is tender. Add undrained cherries. Blend arrowroot with lemon juice and stir into mixture. Bring to boil and simmer for 4 minutes or until sauce has thickened. Serve hot with rice.

Kidneys with Bacon

PREPARATION TIME: 20 minutes

COOKING TIME: 25 minutes

SERVES: 4 people

450g (1lb) lambs' kidneys
1 tbsp tomato chutney
8 rashers streaky bacon, diced
1 onion, peeled and quartered
3 cloves garlic, crushed
30ml (2 tbsps) oil
15ml (1 tbsp) light soy sauce
15ml (1 tbsp) cornflour
45ml (3 tbsps) sherry
15ml (1 tbsp) chopped parsley
30ml (2 tbsps) water
Salt
Pepper

GARNISH
Sprig of parsley

Cut kidneys in half and remove hard core with a sharp knife or scissors. Cut a lattice design on back of kidneys. Pour over sherry, and set aside for 15 minutes. Heat wok and add oil. Add bacon, onion and garlic, and stir-fry for 5 minutes. Remove from wok. Add kidneys, reserving sherry, and fry for 3 minutes. Stir in tomato chutney. Add soy sauce and water to wok, and return bacon and onion mixture. Add salt and pepper to taste. Cover and simmer gently for 10 minutes. Meanwhile, blend cornflour with sherry marinade.

Add parsley and cornflour mixture, and stir, cooking gently until sauce thickens. Garnish with parsley. Serve hot with rice.

Lamb with Cherries (left) and Five-Spice Beef with Broccoli (page 111) (bottom left).

Deep-Fried Pork Meatballs

PREPARATION TIME: 25 minutes

COOKING TIME: about 12 minutes

MAKES: 16 meatballs

450g (1lb) lean pork, coarsley minced
1 small onion, finely chopped
1 green chilli, chopped
Salt and freshly ground black pepper to taste
2.5cm (½ inch) fresh root ginger, peeled and finely chopped
1 egg, beaten
15ml (1 tbsp) cornflour
10ml (2 tsps) dark soy sauce
2 sprigs Chinese parsley, finely chopped
5ml (1 tsp) cooked oil
Oil for deep frying
2 spring onions, chopped (for garnishing)
1 green pepper, seeded and cut into rings (for garnishing)

Mix the minced pork with the chopped onion, chilli, salt and pepper to taste, chopped ginger, beaten egg, cornflour, soy sauce, parsley and cooked oil. Leave to stand for 10 minutes. Form into 16 even-sized balls. Heat the oil in the wok for deep frying and slide a few pork balls into the oil. Fry over a gentle heat for 5-6 minutes, until golden brown and tender. Remove and drain on kitchen paper. Fry all the meatballs and serve with chopped spring onions and green pepper rings sprinkled on top. Serve as a snack, as a starter or as a side dish.

Bean Sprouts with Chopped Pork

PREPARATION TIME: 15 minutes

COOKING TIME: 10 minutes

SERVES: 4 people

225g (½lb) lean pork, chopped finely or coarsely minced

MARINADE
2.5ml (½ tsp) salt
15ml (1 tbsp) light soy sauce
1 egg white, beaten
5ml (1 tsp) cornflour

450g (1lb) bean sprouts
Oil for cooking

SEASONING
2.5ml (½ tsp) salt
2.5ml (½ tsp) sugar
2.5ml (½ tsp) monosodium glutamate (optional)
10ml (2 tsps) soy sauce
5ml (1 tsp) rice wine or dry sherry
15ml (1 tbsp) oyster sauce
2.5cm (½ inch) fresh root ginger, peeled and thinly sliced
2-3 spring onions, chopped
120ml (4 fl oz) chicken stock

SAUCE
2.5ml (½ tsp) cornflour
15ml (1 tbsp) water or stock
Few drops of sesame oil

Mix the pork with the marinade ingredients and keep to one side for 10 minutes. Trim the bean sprouts and chop them coarsely. Heat the wok and 30ml (2 tbsps) oil. Stir-fry the bean sprouts for 1 minute to evaporate excess water and moisture. Remove the bean sprouts and keep on a plate. Mix the seasoning ingredients together. Heat 45ml (3 tbsps) oil in the wok until it smokes. Stir-fry the pork for 2 minutes and then add the ginger, onions and bean sprouts. Stir-fry for 2-3 minutes. Add the seasoning ingredients and stir-fry for 1 minute. Add the chicken stock and the blended sauce ingredients. Cook until the sauce thickens. Serve immediately.

Diced Pork with Walnuts

PREPARATION TIME: 30 minutes

COOKING TIME: 16-18 minutes

SERVES: 3 people

100g (4oz) shelled walnuts
Oil for deep frying

SEASONING
7.5ml (1½ tsps) light soy sauce
Few drops sesame oil
Salt and freshly ground black pepper to taste
15ml (1 tbsp) oil
15ml (1 tbsp) water
15ml (1 tbsp) cornflour
Pinch monosodium glutamate (optional)

225g (½lb) pork fillet, cut into cubes
1 carrot, thinly sliced
1 onion, peeled and cut into pieces
3 spring onions, chopped
2.5cm (1 inch) fresh root ginger, peeled and thinly sliced

SAUCE
90ml (6 tbsps) stock
5ml (1 tsp) cornflour

Cook the walnuts in boiling water for 3-4 minutes. Drain the nuts thoroughly. Deep-fry the walnuts until lightly browned. Remove and drain. Use oil for cooking. Mix the seasoning ingredients together and add the pork. Leave to marinate for 15 minutes. Discard marinade. Heat 30ml (2 tbsps) oil in the wok and stir-fry the carrots for 2 minutes. Add the onions and root ginger and stir-fry for 1 minute. Add 10ml (2 tsps) of the sauce stock and remove to a plate. Add the drained pork cubes and 15ml (1 tbsp) oil to the wok and stir-fry for 4-5 minutes. Mix the remaining stock and the cornflour together for the sauce. Return the walnuts and carrots to the wok, together with the blended sauce ingredients. Mix well and simmer until the sauce thickens. Remove and serve immediately. Serve with rice noodles or fried rice.

Piquant Lambs' Liver

PREPARATION TIME: 15 minutes

COOKING TIME: 20 minutes

SERVES: 4 people

450g (1lb) lambs' liver, cut into thin strips
60g (2oz) butter or margarine
30ml (2 tbsps) wine vinegar
1 onion, peeled and sliced finely
75ml (5 tbsps) white wine
15ml (1 tbsp) chopped parsley
15ml (1 tbsp) flour
Salt
Pepper

GARNISH
Chopped parsley

Combine flour with a good pinch of salt and freshly-ground black pepper. Toss in liver and coat well. Heat wok and add half the butter over gentle

Bean Sprouts with Chopped Pork (top right) and Deep-Fried Pork Meatballs (bottom).

heat. Add onion and fry gently until transparent. Add vinegar and cook over high heat until vinegar has evaporated. Add remaining butter and when hot add liver. Stir-fry briskly for about 3 minutes. Add wine, parsley, and salt and pepper to taste. Bring to the boil and simmer for 5 minutes. Sprinkle with chopped parsley and serve with saffron rice.

Sesame Beef with Dates

PREPARATION TIME: 20 minutes, plus 30 minutes to marinate

COOKING TIME: 12-15 minutes

SERVES: 4 people

SEASONING A
2.5ml (½ tsp) bicarbonate of soda
15ml (1 tbsp) light soy sauce
15ml (1 tbsp) oil
7.5ml (1½ tsps) cornflour

450g (1lb) beef fillet, thinly sliced into 5cm (2-inch) pieces
20 dried dates (red or dark) soaked and stoned

SEASONING B
5ml (1 tsp) monosodium glutamate (optional)
7.5ml (1½ tsps) sugar
10ml (2 tsps) bean paste
200ml (⅓ pint) beef stock, or made with stock cube
Salt to taste
60ml (4 tbsps) cooked oil or plain oil
2.5cm (1 inch) fresh root ginger, peeled and thinly sliced
2 spring onions, sliced

SAUCE
15ml (1 tbsp) cornflour
30ml (2 tbsps) water or stock
30ml (2 tbsps) sesame seeds

Mix the ingredients for Seasoning A. Mix with the beef and marinate for 30 minutes. Drain meat and discard marinade. Drain soaked dates; slice most of them into 4 long pieces, leaving a few whole. Mix the dates with Seasoning B. Heat oil in a wok and stir-fry beef for 4-5 minutes. Add ginger, spring onions, dates and the Seasoning B, and gently bring to the boil. Add the blended sauce ingredients. Cover and simmer for 3-4 minutes over a gentle heat until the sauce thickens and becomes clear. Remove from the heat, place on a serving dish and keep warm. Heat a wok or frying pan and add the sesame seeds. Dry roast for 2 minutes, until they begin to crackle and turn golden brown. Sprinkle over the beef and serve immediately.

Stir Fried Beef with Spring Onions

PREPARATION TIME: 30 minutes

COOKING TIME: 10 minutes

SERVES: 4 people

MARINADE
15ml (1 tbsp) cornflour
1 egg white
15ml (1 tbsp) oil
5ml (1 tsp) bicarbonate of soda
450g (1lb) beef fillet, cut into 2.5cm (1-inch) strips

SEASONING
5ml (1 tsp) Shao Hsing wine
15ml (1 tbsp) light soy sauce
5ml (1 tsp) dark soy sauce
2.5ml (½ tsp) salt
2.5ml (½ tsp) freshly ground black pepper
5ml (1 tsp) monosodium glutamate (optional)

Oil for frying
1 small onion, peeled and thickly sliced
3 spring onions, chopped lengthways
2 leeks, white part only, cut into 4cm (1½-inch) slices
5ml (1 tsp) sesame oil

Mix the marinade ingredients and add the beef strips. Leave to marinate for 20 minutes. Mix all the seasoning ingredients together in a small bowl. Heat 30ml (2 tbsps) oil in a wok and, when it is smoking, add the beef. Reduce the heat and stir-fry for 4-5 minutes. Remove the meat and keep the oil for future use. Heat the wok, add 30ml (2 tbsps) fresh oil and stir-fry the onion and leeks for 2 minutes. Add seasoning mixture and beef, and stir-fry for 1-2 minutes. Sprinkle sesame oil over the top and mix well. Serve immediately. Use as a main dish or side dish.

Shredded Beef with Vegetables

PREPARATION TIME: 15 minutes

COOKING TIME: 10 minutes

SERVES: 2-3 people

225g (8oz) lean beef, cut into thin strips
Pinch salt
60ml (4 tbsps) oil
2 red and green chillies, cut in half then sliced into strips
5ml (1 tsp) black vinegar
1 stem of celery, cut into thin 5cm (2-inch) strips
2 carrots, cut into thin 5cm (2-inch) strips
1 leek, white part only, sliced into thin 5cm (2-inch) strips
2 cloves of garlic, peeled and finely chopped

SEASONING
5ml (1 tsp) light soy sauce
5ml (1 tsp) dark soy sauce
10ml (2 tsps) Shao Hsing wine
5ml (1 tsp) sugar
Pinch monosodium glutamate (optional)
2.5ml (½ tsp) freshly ground black pepper

Put the beef into a bowl and sprinkle with salt; rub salt into meat. Heat 5ml (1 tsp) oil in a wok until it begins to smoke. Reduce heat and add beef and chillies, and stir-fry for 4-5 minutes. Add remaining oil, and stir-fry beef until it turns cripsy. Add vinegar and mix until it evaporates, then add celery, carrots, leek and garlic. Stir-fry for 2 minutes. Mix the seasoning ingredients, pour over the beef and cook for 2 minutes. Serve immediately.

Szechuan Beef

PREPARATION TIME: 20 minutes

MICROWAVE COOKING TIME: 6-18 minutes

SERVES: 4 people

450g (1lb) rump steak, shredded
30ml (2 tbsps) oil
½ dried chilli pepper, crushed
60ml (4 tbsps) soy sauce
120ml (4 fl oz) stock
30ml (2 tbsps) cornflour

Stir-Fried Beef with Onions (top), Shredded Beef with Vegetables (centre left) and Sesame Beef with Dates (bottom).

3 sticks celery, shredded
1 red pepper, shredded

Heat a browning dish for 5 minutes on HIGH. Combine meat and oil and add to the dish. Cook 2 minutes on HIGH in 2 or 3 batches. Re-heat browning dish 2 minutes after each batch. Add the crushed chilli pepper. Mix the soy sauce and stock and gradually stir into the cornflour. Pour over the steak and cook 2-3 minutes. Add the celery and red pepper and mix together with the meat and sauce. Cook a further 1 minute on HIGH until the sauce has thickened but the vegetables are still crisp.

Five-Spice Beef with Broccoli

PREPARATION TIME: 15 minutes

COOKING TIME: 15 minutes

SERVES: 4 people

225g (8oz) fillet or rump steak
1 clove garlic, crushed
2.5ml (½ tsp) finely grated ginger
2.5ml (½ tsp) five-spice powder
115g (4oz) broccoli florets
Bunch of chives, snipped into 2.5cm (1-inch) lengths
30ml (2 tbsps) peanut oil
2.5ml (½ tsp) salt
15ml (1 tbsp) dark soy sauce
½ cup hot water
10ml (2 tsps) cornflour, slaked in 15ml (1 tbsp) cold water

Cut steak into thin slices, then into narrow strips. Mix together with garlic, ginger, and five-spice powder. Heat wok, add 15ml (1 tbsp) oil, and stir-fry broccoli for 8 minutes. Remove broccoli and add remaining oil. Add meat, and stir-fry for 3 minutes. Add broccoli, soy sauce, salt and water, and heat to simmering point. Mix cornflour with cold water, and pour into wok, stirring continuously until liquid thickens. Toss in chives, stir, and serve immediately with boiled rice.

Guy's Curry (Hot)

PREPARATION TIME: 40 minutes

COOKING TIME: 2 hours 15 minutes

SERVES: 4 people

1kg (2lb) steak, skirt or rump, cut into 1.5cm (½-inch) cubes
1½ cups coconut cream
1 onion, peeled and finely chopped
3 cloves garlic, chopped
30ml (2 tbsps) sultanas
15ml (1 tbsp) curry leaves
7.5ml (1½ tsps) cumin
7.5ml (1½ tsps) coriander
15ml (1 tbsp) vindaloo curry paste (or milder curry paste if a curry less hot than vindaloo is desired)
1 carrot, grated
2 apples, chopped finely
1 banana, sliced finely
2 tomatoes, chopped finely
1 red pepper, cored, seeds removed, and chopped finely
6 small pieces lemon rind
30ml (2 tbsps) desiccated coconut
7.5ml (1½ tsps) sugar
1 cup water
150ml (¼ pint) safflower or vegetable oil

ACCOMPANIMENT
1 apple, chopped finely
1 banana, sliced
1 red pepper, cored, seeds removed, and chopped finely
1 carrot, grated
1 tomato, chopped finely
30ml (2 tbsps) sultanas
30ml (2 tbsps) desiccated coconut
Half a cucumber, sliced, in 2 tbsps natural yogurt

Prepare the fruit and vegetables. Heat wok, add oil, and heat until warm. Add onion and garlic, and fry until golden brown. Remove and discard the garlic. Add steak and stir-fry until well browned all over. Add sultanas and stir in well. Add curry leaves, stir in, and cook for 5 minutes. Add cumin and coriander and stir. Cook a further 5 minutes. Add curry paste and cook for 10 minutes. Add grated carrot, red pepper, apples, tomatoes, lemon rind and banana and mix in well. Add water. Cover and cook for 30 minutes. Stir in desiccated coconut and cook for a further 30 minutes. Add sugar and cook for another 20 minutes. Add more water as necessary. Add coconut cream and cook a further 20 minutes. Serve hot with boiled rice and accompaniments.

Peking Sweet Lamb

PREPARATION TIME: 1 hour

MICROWAVE COOKING TIME: 8-9 minutes plus 2 minute standing time

SERVES: 4 people

450g (1lb) lamb fillet or meat from the leg, thinly sliced
30ml (2 tbsps) hoisin sauce
15ml (1 tbsp) rice wine
15ml (1 tbsp) sesame oil
30ml (2 tbsps) sugar
30ml (2 tbsps) light soy sauce
30ml (2 tbsps) vinegar
15ml (1 tbsp) rice wine
15ml (1 tbsp) cornflour
140ml (¼ pint) brown stock
5ml (1 tsp) grated fresh ginger root

GARNISH
4 spring onions, diagonally sliced

Mix the lamb, hoisin sauce and 15ml (1 tbsp) rice wine. Set aside for 1 hour. Combine the sesame oil and sugar in a casserole dish. Heat for 1 minute on HIGH and stir. Add the lamb to the casserole, cover and cook 2 minutes on HIGH. Lower the setting to MEDIUM. Mix the remaining ingredients together, except for the garnish, and pour over the lamb. Cook for 5-7 minutes more, or until lamb is tender. Leave to stand for 2 minutes before serving, garnished with the sliced spring onions.

Right: Guy's Curry (page 111).

Chinese COOKING

POULTRY RECIPES

Roast Crispy Duck

PREPARATION TIME: 15-20 minutes plus 6-8 hours to dry

COOKING TIME: 1 hour 30 minutes

SERVES: 4-6 people

2kg (4½lbs) duck or goose, prepared for cooking
250ml (8 fl oz) water
6 large scallions or 12 spring onions, cut into 5cm (2-inch) lengths
60ml (4 tbsps) maltose or golden syrup
2.5ml (½ tsp) red food colouring
30ml (2 tbsps) tomato purée

Wash the duck and pat it dry on a clean cloth. Ease the fingers between the skin and flesh of the duck, starting at the neck end and working the length of the bird. Put a stick or large skewer through the neck and the cavity of the duck to wedge it securely. This will make the duck easier to handle. Hold the duck over the sink and pour boiling water over it. Pat the duck dry. Melt half the maltose and dissolve in the water. Stand the duck on a rack over a deep tray. Slowly pour the maltose liquid over the duck. Pour the maltose liquid over the duck 3 or 4 times. Leave the duck in a cool place for 6-8 hours, or overnight, until the skin is dry. Remove the stick. Stand the duck on a rack in a roasting tin. Preheat the oven to 200°C, 400°F, Gas Mark 6 and cook for 30 minutes. Turn over and cook the underside for a further 30 minutes. Melt the remaining maltose with the tomato purée and add the food colouring. Spread over the duck and cook for a further 30 minutes. (The duck should have a crisp, red skin.) Remove the duck skin in squares. Slice the duck flesh and serve with the skin on the top. Serve the following dip as an accompaniment.

DUCK DIP
100g (4oz) sugar
60ml (4 tbsps) sweet bean paste
30ml (2 tbsps) sesame oil
120ml (4 fl oz) water

Heat the wok and add the mixed ingredients. Cook for 3-4 minutes until the sugar has dissolved and the dip is smooth. Serve in individual cups.

Sliced Duck with Bamboo Shoots

PREPARATION TIME: 30 minutes

COOKING TIME: 10 minutes

SERVES: 2-3 people

1kg (2¼lb) small duck
5ml (1 tsp) monosodium glutamate (optional)
12.5ml (2½ tsps) cornflour
30ml (2 tbsps) water
100g (4oz) broccoli, chopped
45ml (3 tbsps) oil
2-3 spring onions, chopped
2.5cm (1 inch) fresh root ginger, peeled and thinly sliced
1 clove garlic, peeled and finely chopped
2.5ml (½ tsp) sugar
100g (4oz) bamboo shoots, sliced
Salt and freshly ground black pepper to taste
60ml (4 tbsps) chicken stock
10ml (2 tsps) rice wine or sweet sherry
Few drops sesame oil

Cut the duck flesh into bite-size pieces, removing all the bones. Mix the monosodium glutamate, 7.5ml (1½ tsps) cornflour and 15ml (1 tbsp) water together. Stir in the duck. Marinate for 20 minutes. Cook the broccoli in boiling water for 1 minute. Drain thoroughly. Heat the wok and add the oil. Stir-fry the onions, ginger, garlic and bamboo shoots for 1-2 minutes. Add the duck pieces and stir-fry for 2-3 minutes. Add the sugar, salt and pepper to taste, stock, rice wine and sesame oil. Stir-fry for 3 minutes. Add the remaining cornflour and water blended together. Stir over the heat until the sauce thickens. Serve immediately, as a side dish.

Duck with Ginger and Pineapple

PREPARATION TIME: 20 minutes

COOKING TIME: 2 hours to 2 hours 45 minutes

SERVES: 4-6 people

1.25cm (½ inch) fresh root ginger, peeled and crushed
30ml (2 tbsps) soy sauce
2kg (4½lb) duck
Salt and freshly ground black pepper to taste
45ml (3 tbsps) oil
10cm (4 inches) fresh root ginger, peeled and thinly sliced
50g (2oz) beansprouts
3 spring onions, chopped
2 carrots, peeled, sliced and blanched in boiling water for 2 minutes
10ml (2 tsps) brown sugar
15ml (1 tbsp) wine vinegar
5ml (1 tsp) white vinegar
225g (8oz) can pineapple chunks in syrup
15ml (1 tbsp) cornflour mixed with 30ml (2 tbsps) water

Facing page: Sliced Duck with Bamboo Shoots (top), Duck with Ginger and Pineapple (bottom left) and Roast Crispy Duck (bottom right).

Mix together the crushed ginger, half of the soy sauce and salt and pepper to taste. Wash the duck and pat it dry. Rub the outside of the duck with salt and put on a wire rack in a roasting tin. Roast at 180°C, 350°F, Gas Mark 4 for 30 minutes. Brush the ginger and soy sauce mixture over the duck. Baste frequently with the sauces from the pan and roast for 2 hours, turning the bird occasionally to brown all sides. Remove and slice the duck in small pieces. Heat the oil in a wok and stir-fry the sliced ginger, bean sprouts, onions and carrots for 1-2 minutes. Add the duck slices and cook for 1 minute, then add the brown sugar, vinegar and pineapple chunks in their syrup. Bring to the boil and cook for 2-3 minutes. Add the blended cornflour and cook until the sauce thickens. Serve as a main dish along with noodles or rice.

Empress Chicken

PREPARATION TIME: 30 minutes

MICROWAVE COOKING TIME: 15 minutes plus 3 minutes standing time

SERVES: 4 people

4 chicken wings
4 chicken breasts, skinned
12 dried Chinese mushrooms
120ml (4 fl oz) soy sauce
570ml (1 pint) chicken stock mixed with 45ml (3 tbsps) cornflour
15ml (1 tbsp) sugar
2 pieces star anise
2 slices ginger root
15ml (1 tbsp) rice wine
2.5ml (½ tsp) salt
2 cans bamboo shoots, drained and cut in strips if thick
4 spring onions, sliced

With a heavy cleaver, chop the chicken, through the bones, into large chunks. Remove any splinters of bone. Soak the mushrooms in hot water for 30 minutes. Drain and trim off the stems. Put the chicken, mushrooms and remaining ingredients, except the onions and bamboo shoots, into a deep casserole. Cover well and cook 15 minutes on HIGH or until the chicken is completely cooked. Add the bamboo shoots and sliced onions. Leave to stand 3 minutes and remove star anise before serving.

Chicken and Cashew Nuts

PREPARATION TIME: 15 minutes

COOKING TIME: 15 minutes

SERVES: 4 people

350g (12oz) chicken breast, sliced into 2.5cm (1-inch) pieces
15ml (1 tbsp) cornflour

SEASONING
5ml (1 tsp) salt
5ml (1 tsp) sesame oil
15ml (1 tbsp) light soy sauce
2.5ml (½ tsp) sugar

Oil for deep frying
100g (4oz) cashew nuts
2 spring onions, chopped
1 small onion, peeled and cubed
2.5cm (1 inch) fresh root ginger, peeled and sliced
2 cloves of garlic, sliced
75g (3oz) snow peas (mange tout)
50g (2oz) bamboo shoots, thinly sliced

SAUCE
10ml (2 tsps) cornflour
15ml (1 tbsp) Hoi Sin sauce
250ml (just over ⅓ pint) chicken stock
Pinch monosodium glutamate (optional)

Roll the chicken pieces in cornflour. Discard the remaining cornflour. Mix the seasoning ingredients together and pour over chicken. Leave to stand for 10 minutes. Heat oil for deep frying and fry cashew nuts until golden brown. Remove the nuts and drain on kitchen paper. Heat 30ml (2 tbsps) oil in a wok and stir-fry the onions, ginger and garlic for 2-3 minutes. Add snow peas and bamboo shoots and stir-fry for 3 minutes. Remove the fried ingredients. Add 15ml (1 tbsp) oil to the wok and fry the chicken for 3-4 minutes. Remove the chicken. Clean the wok and add a further 10ml (2 tbsps) oil, and return chicken, cashew nuts and fried onions, etc. to the wok. Prepare the sauce by mixing the cornflour, Hoi Sin sauce, chicken stock and monosodium glutamate together. Pour over the chicken. Mix well and cook until the sauce thickens and becomes transparent. Serve hot with a chow mein dish. Alternatively, a few chunks of pineapple will add extra zest to the dish.

Golden Chicken with Walnuts

PREPARATION TIME: 20 minutes

MICROWAVE COOKING TIME: 7-9 minutes plus 2 minutes standing time

SERVES: 4 people

450g (1lb) chicken, skinned, boned and cut into bite-sized pieces
15ml (1 tbsp) cornflour
15ml (1 tbsp) light soy sauce
15ml (1 tbsp) sherry
280ml (½ pint) stock
1 small can salted yellow beans
90g (3oz) walnuts, roughly chopped
½ small can sliced bamboo shoots

Combine chicken, cornflour, soy sauce, sherry, stock, and yellow beans in a casserole dish. Cover and cook on HIGH for 7-9 minutes, stirring halfway through the cooking time. Once the sauce has thickened, add the walnuts and bamboo shoots. Leave to stand 2 minutes before serving.

Fried Shredded Chicken on Cabbage

PREPARATION TIME: 20 minutes

COOKING TIME: 12 minutes

SERVES: 4 people

450g (1lb) Chinese white cabbage, cut into 2.5cm (1-inch) pieces
Pinch bicarbonate of soda

SEASONING
15ml (1 tbsp) light soy sauce
15ml (1 tbsp) cornflour
1.25ml (¼ tsp) sesame oil
1.25ml (¼ tsp) freshly ground black pepper

Facing page: Empress Chicken (top) and Golden Chicken with Walnuts (bottom).

2.5ml (½ tsp) sugar
2.5ml (½ tsp) salt
15ml (1 tbsp) water
15ml (1 tbsp) oil
Pinch monosodium glutamate (optional)
30ml (2 tbsps) oil
1 onion, peeled and roughly chopped
2.5cm (1 inch) fresh root ginger, peeled and thinly sliced
450g (1lb) boned chicken breasts, shredded
4-6 mushrooms, sliced

SAUCE
45ml (3 tbsps) chicken stock
1.25ml (¼ tsp) sesame oil
5ml (1 tsp) light soy sauce
5ml (1 tsp) cornflour
5ml (1 tsp) monosodium glutamate (optional)

Wash cabbage and blanch in boiling water with a pinch of bicarbonate of soda for 2 minutes. Drain well and keep warm. Mix the seasoning ingredients together. Heat the wok and add the oil. Fry the onions, ginger and chicken for 2-3 minutes. Add the mushrooms and fry for further 2 minutes. Add the stock and cook for 4-5 minutes. Mix the sauce ingredients together and pour over the chicken. Cook for 2 minutes. Meanwhile, place the cabbage on a warmed dish as a bed for the chicken. Serve immediately.

Roast Spiced Duck

PREPARATION TIME: 3-4 hours to dry, and 1 hour to glaze

COOKING TIME: 1 hour

SERVES: 4-6 people

2kg (4½lb) duck or small goose
5ml (1 tsp) five spice powder
7.5ml (1½ tsp) salt
60ml (4 tbsps) maltose or golden syrup
5ml (1 tsp) white vinegar
10ml (2 tsps) malt or red vinegar
Oil

Wash and dry the duck. Rub in the five spice powder and salt. Close the cavities of the duck by securing both ends with small skewers. Mix the

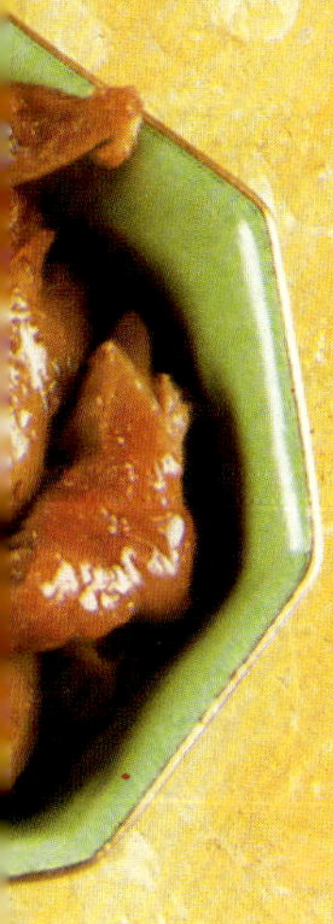

maltose and vinegar together with a little water and bring to the boil. Spoon this liquid over the duck several times, collecting the liquid in a tray. Hang the duck by its neck for 3-4 hours to dry. Preheat the oven to 230°C, 450°F, Gas Mark 8. Place the duck in a roasting tin. Rub oil into the skin. Roast in the oven for 1 hour, basting with any remaining maltose and vinegar liquid.

If the duck is not quite tender, cook for a little longer. Slice the duck onto a warmed serving dish and serve immediately.

Inset far left: Stewed Chicken and Pineapple (page 122) (top right), Fried Shredded Chicken on Cabbage (page 116) (centre left) and Chicken and Cashew Nuts (page 116) (bottom right). Roast Spiced Duck (top left), Roast Peking Duck (page 120) (left) and Steamed Duck in Wine Sauce (bottom).

Steamed Duck in Wine Sauce

PREPARATION TIME: 20 minutes

COOKING TIME: 3 hours 30 minutes

SERVES: 4-6 people

2kg (4½lb) duck
150ml (¼ pint) Kao Liang wine or mild red wine
2.5ml (½ tsp) monosodium glutamate (optional)
2.5cm (1 inch) fresh root ginger, peeled and thinly sliced
3 spring onions, chopped
5ml (1 tsp) salt
5ml (1 tsp) sugar
5ml (1 tsp) cornflour

Place the duck in a large pot. Add water to cover and boil for 5-7 minutes. Remove the duck and drain well. Mix all the remaining ingredients together apart from the cornflour. Place the duck in a deep dish and stand over a steamer. Pour the wine mixture over the duck. Cover and steam for 2-3 hours until the duck is quite tender. Remove the duck and strain the cooking liquid. Place the duck on a serving dish, either whole or cut into slices. Blend the cooking liquid with the cornflour. Bring to the boil and stir until thickened. Pour over the duck. Serve immediately.

Diced Chicken and Peppers

PREPARATION TIME: 20 minutes

MICROWAVE COOKING TIME: 8½-10½ minutes plus 2 minutes standing time

SERVES: 4 people

30ml (2 tbsps) oil
1 clove garlic, minced
450g (1lb) chicken, skinned, boned and diced
2 green peppers, diced
1 small red chilli pepper, diced
½ small can bamboo shoots, diced
5ml (1 tsp) cornflour
30ml (2tbsps) white wine
30ml (2 tbsps) soy sauce
60ml (4 tbsps) chicken stock
Pinch sugar (optional)
Salt

Heat oil for 30 seconds on HIGH in a large casserole dish. Add the garlic and cook 30 seconds on HIGH. Add the chicken and stir to coat with oil. Add the chilli pepper, cornflour, wine, soy sauce and stock. Stir well and cover the dish. Cook 7-9 minutes on HIGH, stirring halfway through the cooking time. Add the green pepper, sugar (if using) and salt if needed. Cook 30 seconds on HIGH, add bamboo shoots and leave to stand, covered, 2 minutes before serving. Serve with fried or plain boiled rice.

Roast Peking Duck

PREPARATION TIME: 15 minutes plus 2-3 hours to dry out the skin

COOKING TIME: 1 hour 20 minutes

SERVES: 4-6 people

2kg (4½lb) duck or small goose
1 litre (1¾ pints) boiling water
30ml (2 tbsps) maltose or golden syrup
250ml (8 fl oz) water
2-3 seedless oranges, peeled and cut into rings
30ml (2 tbsps) oil
Salt and freshly ground black pepper

SAUCE
10ml (2 tsps) cornflour
60ml (4 tbsps) water or stock
Pinch monosodium glutamate (optional)
10ml (2 tsps) light soy sauce
5ml (1 tsp) rice wine or dry sherry

GARNISH
4 spring onions, cut into 5cm (2-inch) lengths

Wash and dry the duck. Put a stick or skewer through the neck and the cavity of the duck so that it is easier to handle. Hold the bird over the sink and pour boiling water over it. Hang the duck up to dry. Melt the maltose and water together and spoon over the duck several times, catching the liquid on a drip tray each time. Leave the duck to dry for 2-3 hours in a cool place. Save any liquid that runs off. Preheat the oven to 200°C, 400°F, Gas Mark 6. Place the duck, breast side down, in a roasting tin and roast for 30 minutes. Lift out the duck, put the orange rings into the tin and place the duck on top, breast side uppermost. Baste with the oil and season with salt and pepper. Roast for a further 45-50 minutes, until tender. Cut off the duck joints and slice the breast meat. Arrange with the orange slices on a serving dish and keep warm.

TO MAKE THE SAUCE
Mix the sauce ingredients together and add any reserved maltose liquid. Bring to the boil gently, stirring until the sauce thickens. Pour over the cooked duck and sprinkle with the onions.

Peking Duck with Pancakes

PREPARATION TIME: for duck 2-3 hours; for pancakes 6 minutes

COOKING TIME: for duck 1 hour 20 minutes; for pancakes 15 minutes

SERVES: 6-8 people

2kg (4½lb) Peking duck (see recipe)
16-20 spring onions, sliced into 7.5cm (3-inch) pieces

PANCAKES (PO PING)
450g (1lb) flour
Pinch salt
15ml (1 tbsp) corn oil
5ml (1 tsp) sesame oil
Tepid water for kneading
Flour for rolling

TO MAKE PANCAKES
Sift the flour and salt into a mixing bowl. Make a well in the centre and add the corn oil and water, a little at a time, and work in the flour. Make a pliable dough. Remove from the bowl and knead well for 2-3 minutes. Cover with a damp, clean cloth and allow to rest for 10 minutes. Knead again for 1 minute and divide the dough into 16-20 even-sized balls. Roll each ball in flour and roll out into a 10-15cm (4-6 inch) circle. Place a frying pan on the heat and, when moderately hot, place the rolled circle of dough on it; cook for ½-1 minute. Little bubbles will appear; flip over and allow to cook for 1-1½ minutes. Pick the pancake up and check whether little brown specks have appeared on the undersides; if not, then cook for a few seconds more. Use a clean tea towel to press the pancakes gently, this will circulate the steam and cook the pancakes. Prepare the rest of the pancakes in the same way and keep them stacked, wrapped in foil to keep them warm.

TO MAKE DIP
60ml (4 tbsps) sugar
60ml (4 tbsps) bean paste (sweet)
15ml (1 tbsp) sesame oil
15ml (1 tbsp) corn oil or peanut oil
120ml (4 fl oz) water

OTHER DIPS, READY PREPARED
60ml (4 tbsps) Hoi Sin sauce
60ml (4 tbsps) Chinese barbecue sauce

Mix together the sugar, bean paste and water. Warm the wok, add the oil and then the sugar mixture. Bring to boil and, when the sugar has melted, remove and put in a bowl. Place the duck on a cutting board and cut thin slices from the breast area and thighs. Place a pancake on an individual plate, cover with a slice of duck and a few strips of onion, spread on a dip of your

Facing page: Diced Chicken and Peppers. This page: Peking Duck with Pancakes.

choice, roll up like a pancake and eat. To make very crisp duck, cut duck into large joints and deep fry till crispy.

Chicken Chow Mein

PREPARATION TIME: 30 minutes

COOKING TIME: 20 minutes

SERVES: 4 people

450g (1lb) egg noodles or spaghetti, broken into small pieces
1 onion, peeled and thinly sliced
50g (2oz) mushrooms, sliced
3 spring onions, chopped
2 cloves of garlic, peeled and chopped
Salt and taste
Pinch monosodium glutamate
60ml (4 tbsps) oil
175g (6oz) chicken meat, finely shredded
30ml (2 tbsps) light soy sauce
5ml (1 tsp) sugar
15ml (1 tbsp) rice wine or dry sherry
90ml (6 tbsps) chicken stock

Cook the noodles in boiling, salted water for 4-5 minutes, until tender. Drain and rinse under cold water. Drain once again and add 30ml (2 tbsps) oil; mix well to prevent the noodles from sticking together. Heat 30ml (2 tbsps) oil in a wok and fry the onions and garlic for 2 minutes. Add chicken and stir-fry for 3-4 minutes. Add mushrooms. Sprinkle over the wine, sugar, soy sauce, monosodium glutamate and salt to taste. Cook until the mixture is fairly dry. Add noodles and stir well to mix. Sprinkle over the stock and cook once again until dry. Serve with chilli sauce and dark soy sauce. 50g (2oz) sliced green beans, 50g (2oz) peas or 50g (2oz) shredded carrot may also be added, along with the chicken pieces.

Stewed Chicken and Pineapple

PREPARATION TIME: 30 minutes

COOKING TIME: 15 minutes

SERVES: 4 people

SEASONING
30ml (2 tbsps) light soy sauce
15ml (1 tbsp) oil
15ml (1 tbsp) cornflour
5ml (1 tsp) salt
2.5ml (½ tsp) sesame oil
30ml (2 tbsps) water
750g (1½lb) boned chicken breast, cut into cubes

SAUCE
7.5ml (1½ tsps) cornflour
250ml (8 fl oz) water or chicken stock
10ml (2 tsps) dark soy sauce
Salt to taste
30ml (2 tbsps) oil
1 onion, peeled and cut into chunks
2 spring onions, finely chopped
2.5cm (1 inch) fresh root ginger, peeled and thinly sliced
4-5 pineapple rings, cut into chunks

Mix the seasoning ingredients together. Add the cubed chicken and marinate for 10-12 minutes. Mix the sauce ingredients together in a bowl. Heat the oil in a wok and fry the onions for 2 minutes until just tender. Add the drained chicken, and fry for 3-4 minutes. Add the root ginger and fry for 1 minute. Add any remaining marinade and the sauce ingredients and bring to the boil. Cook, stirring, until the sauce thickens then add the pineapple chunks. Heat through. Remove from the heat and serve with fried rice.

Tangerine Peel Chicken

PREPARATION TIME: 30 minutes

COOKING TIME: 12-15 minutes

SERVES: 4 people

450g (1lb) boned chicken breast, cut into 2.5cm (1-inch) pieces

SEASONING
2.5ml (½ tsp) salt
7.5ml (1½ tsps) sugar
2.5ml (½ tsp) monosodium glutamate (optional)
5ml (1 tsp) dark soy sauce
10ml (2 tsps) light soy sauce
5ml (1 tsp) rice wine or dry sherry
10ml (2 tsps) malt vinegar
5ml (1 tsp) sesame oil
10ml (2 tsps) cornflour

Oil for deep frying
1-2 red or green chillies, seeded and chopped
1.25cm (½ inch) fresh root ginger, peeled and finely chopped
5cm (2 inches) dried tangerine peel, coarsely ground or crumbled
2 spring onions, finely chopped

SAUCE
2.5ml (½ tsp) cornflour
15-30ml (1-2 tbsps) water or stock

Mix the chicken pieces with the seasoning ingredients and stir well. Leave to marinate for 10-15 minutes. Remove the chicken pieces and reserve the marinade. Heat wok and add the oil for deep frying. Once it starts to smoke add the chicken pieces and fry for 4-5 minutes, until golden. Drain chicken on kitchen paper. Tip off the oil, leaving 15ml (1 tbsp) oil in the wok, and stir-fry the chillies, ginger, tangerine peel and onions for 2-3 minutes. When they begin to colour add the chicken and stir-fry for 1 minute. Mix the reserved marinade with the sauce ingredients and pour over the chicken. Stir and cook for 2-3 minutes, until the sauce thickens and the chicken is tender. Serve immediately.

Sweet and Sour Chicken

PREPARATION TIME: 30 minutes

COOKING TIME: 20 minutes

SERVES: 3-4 people

2.5ml (½ tsp) salt
10ml (2 tsps) cornflour
1 chicken breast, cut into 1cm (½-inch) cubes
1 onion, peeled and roughly chopped into 1cm (½-inch) chunks
25g (1oz) bamboo shoots, sliced
1 green pepper, seeded and thinly sliced
2.5cm (1 inch) fresh root ginger, peeled and thinly sliced
2 carrots, scraped and thinly sliced into 2.5cm (1-inch) long pieces
1 garlic clove, peeled and chopped
30ml (2 tbsps) oil

Facing page: Tangerine Peel Chicken (top), Sweet and Sour Chicken (centre left) and Chicken Chow Mein (bottom).

BATTER
100g (4oz) plain flour
25g (1oz) cornflour
1 small egg
Oil for deep-frying

SAUCE
15ml (1 tbsp) soft brown sugar
15ml (1 tbsp) red wine vinegar or white vinegar
15ml (1 tbsp) soy sauce
15ml (1 tbsp) tomato purée
450ml (¾ pint) chicken stock
Pinch monosodium glutamate (optional)
10ml (2 tsps) cornflour

Mix salt and cornflour and roll chicken pieces in it. Make the batter by mixing the sieved flour and cornflour with the egg and sufficient water to make a thick batter. Beat well. Heat oil for deep frying. Dip the chicken pieces into the batter and deep-fry until golden brown and crisp. Drain on absorbent paper and keep warm. Heat the 30ml (2 tbsps) oil in a wok and stir-fry the onions, ginger and garlic for 2-3 minutes. Add the carrots and fry for 2 minutes. Add the green peppers and fry for 2 minutes. Add the bamboo shoots, season with salt and stir well. Mix all the sauce ingredients together. Pour over the cooked vegetables. Cook for 2-3 minutes, until the sauce thickens. The sauce should become transparent. Arrange fried chicken pieces on a serving dish and pour the sweet and sour sauce over them. Serve as a side dish.

Chicken Fry with Sauce

PREPARATION TIME: 20 minutes

COOKING TIME: about 24 minutes

SERVES: 4 people

15ml (1 tbsp) cooked oil
5ml (1 tsp) sesame oil
25g (1oz) sesame seeds

SAUCE
2 cloves of garlic, minced
2 spring onions, finely chopped or minced
5ml (1 tsp) Chinese black vinegar or brown malt vinegar
45ml (3 tbsps) dark soy sauce
5ml (1 tsp) light soy sauce
2.5ml (½ tsp) monosodium glutamate (optional)
2.5ml (½ tsp) salt
7.5ml (1½ tsps) sugar
8 chicken thighs, or 450g (1lb) chicken, cut into small joints

Heat the wok and add the oils. Stir-fry the sesame seeds till they change colour to golden brown. Remove to a dish. Mix sauce ingredients together and add the sesame seeds. Wipe the wok and add the chicken. Add sufficient water to cover, and cook for 20 minutes, until the chicken is tender. De-bone the

chicken and quickly cut into bite-size pieces. Arrange the chicken on a plate and spoon the sauce over the top. Serve immediately.

Chicken and Mushrooms

PREPARATION TIME: 15 minutes, plus 10 minutes to marinate

COOKING TIME: 10-12 minutes

SERVES: 3-4 people

SEASONING
2.5ml (½ tsp) salt
30ml (2 tbsps) light soy sauce
10ml (2 tsps) cornflour
5ml (1 tsp) rice wine or dry sherry
Pinch monosodium glutamate (optional)

225g (½lb) chicken breast, cut into bite-size pieces

SAUCES
Salt to taste
Freshly ground black pepper to taste
15ml (1 tbsp) light soy sauce
250ml (8 fl oz) chicken stock
10ml (2 tsps) cornflour or arrowroot
5ml (1 tsp) oyster sauce

30ml (2 tbsps) oil
1 onion, peeled and chopped
1 clove of garlic, sliced
1cm (½ inch) fresh root ginger, peeled and thinly sliced
3 dried black mushrooms, soaked and sliced
50g (2oz) open mushrooms, sliced
50g (2oz) button mushrooms, sliced

Mix the seasoning ingredients together. Marinate the chicken in the seasoning mixture for 10 minutes. Mix the sauce

Chicken Fry with Sauce (below left), Chicken Green Chilli (page 133) (below centre) and Chicken and Mushrooms (below right).

ingredients together. Heat the oil in a wok and fry the onion, garlic and ginger for 2-3 minutes. Remove and keep on one side. Fry the drained chicken in the remaining oil for 4 minutes. Add the mushrooms and stir-fry for 1 minute. Add a little extra oil if necessary. Return the fried onion mixture to the wok and stir-fry until well mixed. Pour the blended sauce ingredients into the wok and cook gently until the sauce thickens. Serve piping hot.

Duck with Orange

PREPARATION TIME: 30 minutes

COOKING TIME: 50 minutes

SERVES: 4 people

1 small duck
15g (½ oz) butter or margarine
15ml (1 tbsp) oil
3 oranges
300ml (½ pint) light chicken stock
100ml (⅙ pint) red wine
30ml (2 tbsps) redcurrant jelly
5ml (1 tsp) arrowroot
15ml (1 tbsp) cold water
Salt
Pepper

GARNISH
Watercress
Slivers of orange peel

Pare the rind of 2 oranges and cut into fine shreds. Blanch in hot water and set aside for garnish. Extract juice from 2 oranges. Cut peel and pith from 1 orange, and then slice into rounds, or cut flesh into sections if preferred. Wash duck and dry well with absorbent paper. Heat wok, and add oil and butter. When hot, add duck, and brown all over. Remove from wok and, using poultry shears or a cleaver, cut duck in half lengthways, and then cut each half into 2.5cm (1-inch) strips. Return duck to wok, and add stock, red wine, redcurrant jelly, orange juice and rind, and salt and pepper to taste. Bring to boil, reduce heat, cover and simmer gently for 20 minutes. Add orange slices, and simmer a further 10 minutes, or until duck is cooked. If sauce needs to be thickened, mix arrowroot with cold water and add to sauce. Bring to the boil, and simmer for 3 minutes. Garnish with slivers of orange peel and watercress.

Lacquered Duck with Plum Sauce

PREPARATION TIME: 25 minutes

MICROWAVE COOKING TIME:
43-48 minutes plus 10 minutes standing time

SERVES: 4 people

SAUCE
See Plum Sauce recipe

GLAZE
60ml (4 tbsps) honey
60ml (4 tbsps) soy sauce

2.5kg (5lb) duckling

This page: Duck with Orange. Facing page: Lacquered Duck with Plum Sauce.

GARNISH
60g (2oz) toasted, chopped almonds
Spring onion brushes (see Introduction)

Brush the duckling with the honey and soy sauce glaze. Cook on rack on HIGH for 10 minutes. Turn over, brush with the glaze and cook 10 minutes on HIGH. Turn again and brush with some of the plum sauce. Lower the setting to MEDIUM and cook 15-30 minutes, or until tender. Cover and leave to stand 10 minutes before cutting into 8 pieces with a cleaver or poultry shears. Pour over remaining plum sauce and sprinkle over the almonds. Garnish with onion brushes and serve with rice.

Chicken with Mangetout

PREPARATION TIME: 20 minutes

MICROWAVE COOKING TIME: 8½-9½ minutes plus 2 minutes standing time

SERVES: 4 people

30ml (2 tbsps) oil
450g (1lb) chicken breasts, skinned, boned and cut into thin slivers
10ml (2 tsps) cornflour
45ml (3 tbsps) rice wine
45ml (3 tbsps) light soy sauce
30ml (2 tbsps) oyster sauce
60ml (4 tbsps) chicken stock
120g (4oz) mangetout
Dash sesame oil
Salt and pepper

Heat the oil for 30 seconds on HIGH in a large casserole dish. Mix the remaining ingredients, except the mangetout, and pour over the chicken. Cover and cook 7-9 minutes on HIGH, stirring halfway through the cooking time. Add the mangetout, re-cover the dish and cook 30 seconds on HIGH. Leave to stand for 2 minutes before serving. Serve with rice.

Chicken with Hoisin Sauce and Cashews

PREPARATION TIME: 20 minutes

MICROWAVE COOKING TIME: 7-9 minutes plus 2 minutes standing time

SERVES: 4 people

450g (1lb) chicken, skinned, boned and cut into bite-sized pieces
15ml (1 tbsp) cornflour
280ml (½ pint) stock
15ml (1 tbsp) light soy sauce
1 clove garlic, finely minced
15ml (1 tbsp) white wine
60ml (4 tbsps) hoisin sauce
60g (2oz) roasted cashew nuts
4 spring onions, diagonally sliced

Combine the chicken with all the ingredients except the nuts and onions. Put into a casserole dish, cover and

This page: Sesame Chicken with Garlic Sauce (page 130) (top) and Lemon Chicken (page 138) (bottom). Facing page: Chicken with Mangetout (top) and Chicken with Hoisin Sauce and Cashews (bottom).

cook on HIGH for 7-9 minutes, stirring halfway through the cooking time. Once the sauce has thickened and the cornflour has cleared, add the nuts and the spring onions. Re-cover the dish and leave to stand 2 minutes before serving. Serve with rice.

Steamed Chicken

PREPARATION TIME: 20-30 minutes

COOKING TIME: 15-20 minutes

SERVES: 4 people

750g (1½lb) boned chicken

SEASONING
15ml (1 tbsp) light soy sauce
5ml (1 tsp) brown sugar
5ml (1 tsp) salt
15ml (1 tbsp) cornflour
30ml (2 tbsps) oil or cooked oil
2.5ml (½ tsp) monosodium glutamate (optional)
100g (4oz) dried mushrooms, soaked in boiling water for 5 minutes and sliced, or ordinary mushrooms
1cm (½ inch) fresh root ginger, peeled and sliced
4 spring onions, finely chopped
30ml (2 tbsps) stock or water, if needed

Cut the chicken into 2.5cm (1-inch) pieces. Mix the seasoning ingredients together and mix with the chicken. Leave to marinate for 15 minutes. Place a plate in a steamer and put the chicken, mushrooms, ginger, half the onion and the stock on top. Steam over boiling water for 15-20 minutes. Serve with the remaining onions sprinkled over the chicken. The steaming can also be done on a greased lotus leaf or a banana leaf. The flavour is quite stunning.

Sesame Chicken with Garlic Sauce

PREPARATION TIME: 30 minutes

MICROWAVE COOKING TIME:
7-9 minutes plus 2 minutes standing time

SERVES: 4 people

6 chicken thighs, skinned
15ml (1 tbsp) sesame oil
4 cloves garlic, finely minced
5ml (1 tsp) finely chopped ginger root
7.5ml (1½ tsps) brown sugar
30ml (2 tbsps) dark soy sauce
120ml (4 fl oz) chicken stock
2.5ml (½ tsp) black pepper
10ml (2 tsps) cornflour
6 spring onions, sliced
60ml (4 tbsps) sesame seeds
Salt

Bone the chicken thighs and cut the meat into thin strips or small pieces. Combine the garlic, sesame oil, ginger root, sugar, soy sauce and pepper and pour over the chicken in a shallow dish. Cover and refrigerate for 30 minutes. Mix the cornflour and stock, add to the chicken and marinade and stir well. Cover the dish and cook on HIGH for 4-9 minutes, stirring halfway through the cooking time. Add the sesame seeds and onions and leave to stand, covered, 2 minutes before serving. Serve with rice or Chinese noodles.

Chicken Chop Suey

PREPARATION TIME: 30 minutes

COOKING TIME: 15 minutes

SERVES: 4 people

30ml (2 tbsps) light soy sauce
5ml (1 tsp) brown sugar
Salt to taste
450g (1lb) boned chicken, cut into 2.5cm (1-inch) pieces
30ml (2 tbsps) cooking oil
1 onion, cut into chunks
225g (8oz) bean sprouts
10ml (2 tsps) sesame oil
1.25g (¼ tsp) monosodium glutamate (optional)
15ml (1 tbsp) cornflour
250ml (8 fl oz) chicken stock

Mix the soy sauce with the sugar and salt and add the chicken pieces. Allow to marinate for 5 minutes. Drain the chicken and reserve the marinade. Heat the wok and add the oil. Fry the chicken for 2-3 minutes. Remove the chicken. Fry the onions for 2-3 minutes and add the beansprouts. Stir-fry for 4-5 minutes. Return the chicken to the pan and add the sesame oil. Dissolve the monosodium glutamate and the cornflour in the stock and pour over the chicken mixture along with the reserved marinade. Cook for 2-3 minutes, stirring, until the sauce thickens.

Deep-Fried Crispy Chicken

PREPARATION TIME: 3 hours

COOKING TIME: 13-14 minutes

SERVES: 4 people

1.5kg (3-3½lb) chicken, prepared for cooking

SEASONING
5ml (1 tsp) salt
2.5ml (½ tsp) five spice powder
40g (1½oz) maltose
30ml (2 tbsps) malt vinegar
150ml (¼ pint) white vinegar
Oil for deep frying

Wash the chicken and hang it up by a hook to drain and dry. The skin will dry quickly. Pour boiling water over the chicken 4-5 times, to partially cook the skin. This will make the skin crisp during frying. Rub salt and five spice powder well inside the chicken cavity. Dissolve the maltose and vinegars in a pan over a gentle heat. Pour over the chicken. Repeat several times, catching the maltose solution in a drip tray. Leave the chicken to hang and dry for 1½-2 hours, until the skin is smooth and shiny. Heat the oil for deep frying. Deep-fry the chicken for 10 minutes. Ladle hot oil carefully over the chicken continually, until the chicken is deep brown in colour – the skin will puff out slightly. Cook for a further 3-4 minutes and remove from the oil. Drain on absorbent paper. Cut into small pieces and serve with a dip.

Facing page: Chicken Chop Suey (top left), Steamed Chicken (centre right) and Deep-Fried Crispy Chicken (bottom left).

Chicken with Mango (above) and Stir-Fried Chicken with Yellow Bean Paste (bottom right).

Stir-Fried Chicken with Yellow Bean Paste

PREPARATION TIME: 1 hour 10 minutes

COOKING TIME: 20 minutes

SERVES: 4 people

450g (1lb) chicken breasts, sliced thinly
30ml (2 tbsps) oil
30ml (2 tbsps) yellow bean paste
5ml (1 tsp) sugar
1 egg white, lightly beaten
15ml (1 tbsp) rice vinegar
15ml (1 tbsp) light soy sauce
15ml (1 tbsp) cornflour
Salt
Pepper

GARNISH
Spring onion flowers (cut spring onions into 5cm (2-inch) lengths. Carefully cut into fine shreds, keeping one end intact, and then soak in cold water until curling).

Mix together lightly beaten egg white, cornflour, and salt and pepper. Place chicken in a bowl and pour over mixture. Toss together to coat well. Set aside in a cool place for at least 1 hour. Combine vinegar, soy sauce and sugar. Remove chicken, and set egg mixture aside. Heat wok, and add oil. When hot, stir-fry chicken until lightly browned. Remove from wok. Add bean paste to wok and stir-fry for 1 minute. Add vinegar mixture and stir in well. Return chicken to pan, and fry gently for 2 minutes. Finally, add egg mixture, and simmer until sauce thickens, stirring all the time. Garnish with spring onion flowers. Serve immediately with boiled rice.

Chicken with Mango

PREPARATION TIME: 5 minutes

COOKING TIME: 30 minutes

SERVES: 4 people

4 chicken breasts, cut into shreds
2 ripe mangoes, sliced, or 1 can sliced mangoes, drained
4 spring onions, sliced diagonally
2.5ml (½ tsp) ground cinnamon
5ml (1 tsp) grated ginger
15ml (1 tbsp) light soy sauce
1 chicken stock cube
150ml (¼ pint) water
30ml (2 tbsps) oil
30ml (2 tbsps) sweet sherry
5ml (1 tsp) sugar
Salt
Pepper

Heat wok and add oil. Add ginger and cinnamon, and fry for 30 seconds. Add chicken and spring onions, and stir-fry for 5 minutes. Add soy sauce, crumbled chicken stock cube, water and sugar, and bring to boil. Add salt and pepper to taste, and simmer for 15 minutes. Add mangoes and sherry, and simmer, uncovered, until sauce has reduced and thickened. Serve hot with boiled rice.

Chicken Green Chilli

PREPARATION TIME: 10 minutes, plus 10 minutes to marinate

COOKING TIME: 10 minutes

SERVES: 4 people

SAUCE
5ml (1 tsp) light soy sauce
5ml (1 tsp) dark soy sauce
Salt to taste
10ml (2 tsps) cornflour
5ml (1 tsp) sesame oil
5ml (1 tsp) malt vinegar
250ml (8 fl oz) chicken stock

SEASONING
Salt to taste
Freshly ground black pepper to taste
Pinch monosodium glutamate (optional)
30ml (2 tbsps) dark soy sauce
15ml (1 tbsp) light soy sauce
5ml (1 tsp) cornflour
10ml (2 tsps) rice wine or dry sherry

450g (1lb) boned chicken, cut into bite-size pieces
45ml (3 tbsps) oil
3 spring onions, chopped
2.5cm (1 inch) fresh root ginger, peeled and sliced
2 cloves of garlic, peeled and sliced
1 green pepper, seeded and chopped

This page: Duck with Pineapple (page 140). Facing page: Singapore Chicken.

2-3 green chillies, sliced lengthways

Mix the sauce ingredients together. Mix the seasoning ingredients together and add the chicken. Marinate for 10 minutes. Drain the chicken and discard the liquid. Heat 15ml (1 tbsp) oil and stir-fry the onions, ginger and garlic for 2 minutes. Remove to a dish. Add the remaining oil and stir-fry the chicken for 3 minutes. Add the blended green peppers and chillies and stir-fry for 2 minutes. Add the onion mixture and the well-blended sauce ingredients and cook for 3-4 minutes, until the sauce thickens. Serve immediately.

Singapore Chicken

PREPARATION TIME: 20 minutes

MICROWAVE COOKING TIME: 11 minutes plus 2 minutes standing time

SERVES: 4 people

30ml (2 tbsps) oil
10ml (2 tsps) curry powder

Chilli Sichuan Chicken (top) and Honey Soy Chicken Wings (page 138) (bottom). Facing page: Duck with Five Spices (page 140) (top) and Duck with Onions (page 138) (bottom).

450g (1lb) chicken, skinned, boned and cut into bite-sized pieces
1 large onion, cut in large pieces
1 230g (8oz) can pineapple chunks, juice reserved
1 300g (10oz) can mandarin orange segments, juice reserved
15ml (1 tbsp) cornflour
60g (2oz) bean sprouts
Dash soy sauce
Salt and pepper

Heat the oil in a large casserole dish for 30 seconds on HIGH. Add the curry powder, and cook 30 seconds on HIGH. Add the chicken, cover the dish and cook 5 minutes on HIGH. Add the onion, mix the cornflour with the reserved pineapple and orange juice and add to the chicken. Cover and cook 5 minutes on HIGH, stirring occasionally after 1 minute. When the sauce thickens, add the pineapple, orange segments and bean sprouts. Leave to stand 2 minutes before serving. Serve with fried or plain boiled rice.

Chilli Sichuan Chicken

PREPARATION TIME: 40 minutes

COOKING TIME: 20 minutes

SERVES: 4 people

4 chicken breasts, sliced thinly
1 clove garlic, crushed
1 green pepper, cored, seeds removed, and diced
1 red pepper, cored, seeds removed, and diced
1 red chilli, seeds removed, and sliced finely
1 green chilli, seeds removed, and sliced finely
5ml (1 tsp) chilli sauce
15ml (1 tbsp) light soy sauce
5ml (1 tsp) Chinese wine, or dry sherry
2.5ml (½ tsp) cornflour
Salt
Pepper
150ml (¼ pint) peanut oil, for deep frying

SAUCE
300ml (½ pint) chicken stock
10ml (2 tsps) cornflour
5ml (1 tsp) Chinese wine, or dry sherry

Mix together 5ml (1 tsp) wine, ½ tsp cornflour, light soy sauce, and a pinch of salt and pepper. Pour over chicken and mix well. Leave to marinate for at least 30 minutes. Heat oil for deep frying in wok. When hot, toss in sliced

chicken and fry until just colouring and cooked through. Drain well. Carefully remove all but 15ml (1 tbsp) of oil from wok. Heat, and when hot, add garlic, green and red peppers, green and red chillies, and chilli sauce. Fry gently for 2 minutes. Stir 30ml (2 tbsps) of chicken stock into cornflour, then pour remaining chicken stock and wine into wok. Add cornflour mixture and stir well, until sauce boils and thickens. Add chicken, and toss until heated through. Serve with rice.

Lemon Chicken

PREPARATION TIME: 30 minutes

MICROWAVE COOKING TIME: 7-9 minutes plus 2 minutes standing time

SERVES: 4 people

4 chicken breasts, skinned, boned and cut into thin strips
60ml (4 tbsps) soy sauce
10ml (2 tsps) dry sherry or shao-hsing wine
Salt and pepper

SAUCE
45ml (3 tbsps) salted black beans
30ml (2 tbsps) water
90ml (6 tbsps) lemon juice
280ml (8 fl oz) chicken stock
60ml (4 tbsps) sugar
5ml (1 tsp) sesame oil
30ml (3 tbsps) cornflour
2 cloves garlic, finely minced
1.25ml (¼ tsp) red pepper flakes

GARNISH
Lemon slices

Mix chicken with marinade ingredients, cover and refrigerate 30 minutes. Crush the black beans, combine with the water and leave to stand until ready to use. Combine remaining sauce ingredients in a shallow dish. Add the chicken, marinade and black beans, cover and cook on HIGH for 7-9 minutes, stirring halfway through the cooking time. Once the cornflour has cleared, leave the chicken to stand, covered, for 2 minutes before serving. Garnish with lemon slices and serve with rice.

Honey Soy Chicken Wings

PREPARATION TIME: 5 minutes

COOKING TIME: 30 minutes

SERVES: 4 people

450g (1lb) chicken wings
2.5ml (½ tsp) salt
30ml (2 tbsps) peanut oil
60ml (4 tbsps) light soy sauce
30ml (2 tbsps) clear honey
1 clove garlic, crushed
5ml (1 tsp) ginger, freshly grated
5ml (1 tsp) sesame seeds

Heat wok, add oil, and when hot, add chicken wings and fry for 10 minutes. Pour off excess oil carefully. Add soy sauce, honey, sesame seeds, garlic, grated ginger and salt. Reduce heat, and gently simmer for 20 minutes, turning occasionally. Serve hot or cold with rice.

Duck with Onions

PREPARATION TIME: 20 minutes

MICROWAVE COOKING TIME: 42-58 minutes plus 10 minutes standing time

SERVES: 4 people

2.5kg (5lb) duck
90ml (3 fl oz) soy sauce
2 pieces fresh ginger root, peeled and grated
45ml (3 tbsps) white wine
15ml (1 tbsp) sugar
30ml (2 tbsps) cornflour dissolved in 30ml (2 tbsps) water
10 spring onions
1 small can sliced bamboo shoots
4 Chinese mushrooms, soaked and sliced
Salt

Combine the soy sauce and grated ginger and brush over the breast side of the duck. Place the duck on a rack and cook for 10 minutes on HIGH. Turn over, brush with the soy sauce and cook 10 minutes on HIGH. Place in a very large casserole or bowl. Add 3 spring onions, wine and 280ml (½ pint) water. Cover the bowl or casserole and cook 15-30 minutes or until tender. Remove the duck and keep warm. Discard the cooked onions. Skim off fat from the cooking liquid and mix a spoonful of the liquid with the cornflour, water and the sugar. Add the bamboo shoots, mushrooms and remaining onions, sliced, to the sauce. Cook for 2-3 minutes on HIGH until thick and clear. Cut the duck into 8 pieces and pour over the sauce to serve.

Chicken Livers with Peppers

PREPARATION TIME: 30 minutes

COOKING TIME: 15 minutes

SERVES: 4 people

450g (1lb) chicken livers
4 Chinese mushrooms
1 green pepper
1 red pepper
15ml (1 tbsp) rice vinegar
10ml (2 tsps) sugar
30g (1oz) fresh ginger
1 small leek
45ml (3 tbsps) vegetable oil
1 onion

GARNISH
2 spring onion flowers (trim and slice lengthways, keep one end intact, and leave in cold water in refrigerator until curling)

Soak mushrooms in hot water for 20 minutes. Clean and trim chicken livers, and blanch in boiling water for 3 minutes. Drain and slice. Peel and finely slice ginger. Mix together the vinegar and sugar, add ginger, and set aside. Clean and trim leek and cut into thin rings. Peel and slice onion and cut into strips. Core and remove seeds from peppers, and cut into strips. Drain mushrooms, remove hard stalks, and cut caps into thin slices. Heat wok, add oil, and, when hot, add mushrooms, onion, leek and peppers, and stir-fry for 5 minutes. Remove and set aside. Add liver and ginger mixture. Stir-fry for a further 5 minutes, return vegetable mixture to wok and heat through. Serve garnished with spring onion flowers.

Facing page: Chicken Livers with Peppers.

Sesame Fried Chicken

PREPARATION TIME: 10 minutes

COOKING TIME: 30 minutes

SERVES: 4 people

450g (1lb) chicken breasts, or 4 good-sized pieces
115g (4oz) plain flour
5ml (1 tsp) salt
5ml (1 tsp) pepper
60g (2oz) sesame seeds
10ml (2 tsps) paprika
1 egg, beaten, with 15ml (1 tbsp) water
45ml (3 tbsps) olive oil

Sift flour onto a sheet of grease-proof paper and stir in salt, pepper, paprika and sesame seeds. Dip chicken breasts in egg and water mixture, then coat well in seasoned flour. Heat wok, add oil and, when hot, fry the chicken breasts until golden brown on both sides. Turn heat down, and cook gently for 10 minutes on each side. Serve hot with rice.

Duck with Five Spices

PREPARATION TIME: 20 minutes

MICROWAVE COOKING TIME: 30 minutes

SERVES: 4 people

2.5kg (5lb) duckling
140ml (¼ pint) rice wine
140ml (¼ pint) light soy sauce
30ml (2 tbsps) honey
1 clove garlic, finely minced
15ml (1 tbsp) five-spice powder
60ml (4 tbsps) chicken stock
30ml (2 tbsps) cornflour dissolved in 45ml (3 tbsps) water

Remove the meat from the legs and breast of the duck. Take off the skin and cut the meat into bite-sized pieces. Combine with the remaining ingredients, except the cornflour and water, in a casserole. Cover the dish and cook on HIGH for 10 minutes. Reduce the setting and cook an additional 20 minutes on MEDIUM. Check the level of liquid from time to time and add more stock or water if necessary. When the duck is cooked, add a few spoonfuls of the cooking liquid to the cornflour and water. Return the mixture to the casserole and cook on HIGH for 2-3 minutes to thicken the sauce. Serve with rice or stir-fried vegetables. Garnish with Chinese parsley if desired.

Duck with Pineapple

PREPARATION TIME: 20 minutes

MICROWAVE COOKING TIME: 9-10 minutes

SERVES: 4 people

SAUCE
See Pineapple Sauce recipe

2.5kg (5lb) duckling
30ml (2 tbsps) oil
30ml (2 tbsps) soy sauce

GARNISH
4 chives, shredded

Skin the duck and remove the leg and breast meat. Cut into thin slivers. Heat a browning dish 5 minutes on HIGH. Toss the oil and duck together, and add to the browning dish. Cook, uncovered, 4 minutes on HIGH. Add the soy sauce, cover the dish and reduce the setting to MEDIUM. Cook a further 3 minutes, or until duck is tender. Remove duck to a serving dish and keep warm. Coat with the pineapple sauce and sprinkle on the chives. Serve with rice.

Chicken Curry (Mild)

PREPARATION TIME: 10 minutes

COOKING TIME: 40 minutes

SERVES: 4 people

1.5 kgs (3lbs) chicken
15ml (1 tbsp) peanut oil
1 onion, peeled and finely chopped
2 cloves garlic, crushed
2.5ml (½ tsp) grated ginger
10ml (2 tsps) curry powder
2.5ml (½ tsp) salt
15ml (1 tbsp) vinegar
150ml (¼ pint) milk
150ml (¼ pint) coconut cream

Cut chicken into small pieces: breast-meat into 4 pieces, thigh-meat into 2 pieces, and wings separated at joints. Heat oil until hot. Reduce heat, add onion, garlic and ginger, and cook gently, stirring continuously. Cook for 10 minutes, or until onion is soft and a golden brown. Increase heat and add curry powder. Fry for 30 seconds. Add salt and vinegar, and cook for 1 minute. Add chicken, and turn so that mixture coats chicken well. Add coconut cream and milk, and simmer gently over a low heat for 20 minutes. Serve with boiled rice.

Facing page: Chicken Curry (top) and Sesame Fried Chicken (bottom).

VEGETABLES AND SAUCES

Asparagus Salad

PREPARATION TIME: 15 minutes

MICROWAVE COOKING TIME: 5-6 minutes

SERVES: 4 people

450g (1lb) fresh asparagus
45ml (3 tbsps) soy sauce
10ml (2 tsps) sesame oil
15ml (1 tbsp) sesame seeds

Trim the ends of the asparagus spears, wash and drain well. Cut on the diagonal into 3.75cm (1½-inch) lengths, leaving the tips whole. Put into a casserole dish with 120ml (4 fl oz) water. Cook, covered, for 5-6 minutes on HIGH. The asparagus should remain crisp. Mix the soy sauce and sesame oil. Drain the asparagus well and toss with the soy sauce mixture. Sprinkle over the sesame seeds and serve hot or cold.

Steamed Aubergines

PREPARATION TIME: 30 minutes

MICROWAVE COOKING TIME: 6-8 minutes

SERVES: 4 people

1 large or 2 small aubergines
15ml (1 tbsp) sesame oil
45ml (3 tbsps) rice vinegar or white wine vinegar
45ml (3 tbsps) light brown sugar
30ml (2 tbsps) light soy sauce
15ml (1 tbsp) fresh ginger root, grated
1 clove garlic, minced
Salt

Cut off the stems of the aubergines and then cut them in half, lengthwise. Lightly score the surface of each half and sprinkle with salt. Leave to stand for 30 minutes. Combine the remaining ingredients in a glass measure. Cook for 1 minute on HIGH to dissolve sugar. Stir well and set aside to allow flavours to blend. Wash the aubergines and dry well. Cut in quarters, lengthwise, and then into 2.5cm (1-inch) wedges. Put into a casserole dish with 120ml (4 fl oz) water. Cover and cook 5-7 minutes or until just tender. Stir several times during cooking. Drain well. Pour over the sauce and serve hot or cold.

Mangetout with Water Chestnuts

PREPARATION TIME: 15 minutes

MICROWAVE COOKING TIME: 4 minutes

SERVES: 4 people

225g (8oz) mangetout, stems trimmed off
30ml (2 tbsps) oil
Pinch sugar
Pinch salt
1 small can water chestnuts, sliced in rounds
60ml (4 tbsps) light stock
7.5ml (1½ tsps) cornflour
Dash sesame oil

Heat a browning dish for 5 minutes on HIGH. Pour in the oil and add the mangetout. Add the salt and sugar and cook 2 minutes on HIGH, stirring frequently. Add the water chestnuts, cover, and set aside while preparing the sauce. Combine the stock and cornflour in a glass measure. Cook for 2 minutes on HIGH, stirring once, until thickened. Add the sesame oil and mix with the vegetables to serve.

Ginger Dip

PREPARATION TIME: 5 minutes

COOKING TIME:

MAKES: about ½ cup

120ml (4 fl oz) white malt vinegar
2 spring onions, chopped
2.5cm (1 inch) fresh root ginger, peeled and thinly sliced

Mix all the ingredients together and leave for 10-15 minutes before using.

Plum Sauce

PREPARATION TIME: 10 minutes plus soaking overnight

COOKING TIME: 20-25 minutes

MAKES: about 3 cups

225g (8oz) dried apricot
225g (8oz) golden plums, fresh or canned, pitted
50g (2oz) raisins or sultanas
2.5cm (1 inch) fresh root ginger, peeled and shredded
175-225g (6-8oz) sugar
60ml (4 tbsps) white vinegar
2-3 dried red chillies
5ml (1 tsp) salt

Soak apricots overnight in sufficient water to completely cover. Drain apricots and reserve liquid. Mix apricots, plums, sultanas, ginger and sugar and add 250ml (8 fl oz) reserved apricot liquid. Bring to the boil and lower heat to a gentle simmer. Simmer

Facing page: Asparagus Salad (top) and Steamed Aubergines (bottom).

This page: Pea Pods with Water Chestnuts (page 142). Facing page: Green Chilli and Ginger Dip (top), Garlic Dip (page 148) (centre left) and Plum Sauce (page 142) (bottom right).

for 10-15 minutes until it is thick. Add vinegar and coarsely ground chillies to the sauce. Add salt and mix well to blend fruits. Cook for 5-10 minutes until thick and sticky. Cool and bottle.

Green Chilli and Ginger Dip

PREPARATION TIME: 5 minutes

COOKING TIME:

MAKES: about ⅓ cup

4-5 green chillies, chopped
2.5cm (1 inch) fresh root ginger, peeled and finely sliced
2.5ml (½ tsp) salt
2.5m. (½ tsp) sugar
90ml (6 tbsps) malt vinegar

Mix above ingredients together and allow to stand for 2-3 hours before use.

Szechuan Aubergine

PREPARATION TIME: 15 minutes

COOKING TIME: 18-20 minutes

SERVES: 3-4 people

Oil

This page: Bamboo Shoots with Green Vegetables (page 151) (top right), Sweet and Sour Cabbage (page 148) (centre left) and Szechuan Eggplant (page 144) (bottom). Facing page: Sweet-Sour Cabbage.

1 large aubergine, cut into 5cm (2-inch) long and 1cm (½-inch) thick strips
3 cloves garlic, peeled and finely sliced
2.5cm (1 inch) fresh root ginger, peeled and shredded
1 onion, peeled and finely chopped
2 spring onions, chopped
100g (4oz) cooked and shredded chicken
1 red or green chilli, cut into strips

SEASONING
120ml (4 fl oz) chicken stock
5ml (1 tsp) sugar
5ml (1 tsp) red vinegar or wine vinegar
2.5ml (½ tsp) salt
2.5ml (½ tsp) freshly ground black pepper

SAUCE
5ml (1 tsp) cornflour
15ml (1 tbsp) water
5ml (1 tsp) sesame oil

Heat the wok and add 45ml (3 tbsps) oil. Add the aubergine and stir-fry for 4-5 minutes. The aubergine will absorb a lot of oil; keep stirring or else it will burn. Remove from wok and keep on one side. Heat the wok and add 30ml (2 tbsps) oil. Add the garlic and ginger and fry for 1 minute. Add the onions and fry for 2 minutes. Add the chicken and chilli, and cook for 1 minute. Return the aubergine to the wok. Add the blended seasoning ingredients and simmer for 6-7 minutes. Stir in the blended sauce ingredients and simmer until the sauce thickens. Serve with extra sesame oil if desired. This dish goes well with Yung Chow fried rice or rice supreme.

Sweet-Sour Cabbage

PREPARATION TIME: 20 minutes

MICROWAVE COOKING TIME: 11-13 minutes

SERVES: 4 people

1 medium head white cabbage, about 900g (2lbs)
1 small red chilli pepper (use less if desired)
120g (4oz) light brown sugar
90ml (3 fl oz) rice vinegar
30ml (2 tbsps) light soy sauce
Salt
45ml (3 tbsps) oil

Cut the cabbage into 1.25cm (½-inch) slices, discarding the core. Cut the chilli pepper into thin, short strips, discarding the seeds. Mix all the ingredients together, except the oil. Pour the oil into a large bowl and heat

for 2 minutes on HIGH. Add the cabbage and the liquid and cover the bowl with pierced cling film. Cook on HIGH for 9-11 minutes. Allow to cook in the bowl, stirring frequently. When cold, refrigerate. Keeps several days.

Sweet and Sour Cabbage

PREPARATION TIME: 10 minutes

COOKING TIME: 10 minutes

SERVES: 4 people

450g (1lb) white cabbage, shredded
2.5ml (½ tsp) bicarbonate of soda
5ml (1 tsp) salt
10ml (2 tsp) sugar
15ml (1 tbsp) oil

SAUCE
30ml (2 tbsps) sugar
30ml (2 tbsps) wine vinegar
250ml (8 fl oz) chicken stock or water
Pinch salt
15ml (1 tbsp) cornflour or arrowroot
Few drops red food colouring
5ml (1 tsp) tomato purée

Boil the cabbage in a large pan of water with the bicarbonate of soda, salt and sugar for 2-3 minutes. Drain the cabbage and discard the boiling water. Keep the cabbage in cold water for 5 minutes. Drain and keep on one side. Heat the wok and add the oil. Fry the cabbage until it is heated through. Remove to a serving dish. Add the well-stirred sauce ingredients to the wok and gently bring to the boil, stirring. Stir over the heat until the sauce thickens. Pour over the cabbage and serve immediately.

Chilli Oil Dip

PREPARATION TIME: 5-8 minutes

COOKING TIME: 5 minutes

MAKES: about ⅓ cup

60ml (4 tbsps) cooking oil
2 cloves of garlic, bruised
3-4 coarsely ground dried red chillies
30ml (2 tbsps) sesame oil

Heat the cooking oil and fry garlic till dark brown. Remove garlic and discard. Add chillies and fry for a few seconds. Add sesame oil and remove from heat. Stir well and cool.

Garlic Dip

PREPARATION TIME: 5 minutes

COOKING TIME:

MAKES: about ⅓ cup

45ml (3 tbsps) white vinegar
15ml (1 tbsp) minced garlic
Pinch sugar

Mix all the ingredients together and leave for 2 hours before using.

Soy Dip

PREPARATION TIME: 5 minutes

Facing page left: Sweet and Sour Sauce (page 160) (top), Soy Dip (centre) and Chilli Oil Dip (bottom). Facing page right: Hoi Sin Sauce (top), Chilli Sauce (centre) and Ginger Dip (page 142) (bottom). This page: Lettuce and Bean Sprouts with Soy Sauce (left), Braised Aubergine and Chicken with Chilli (page 150) (centre) and Braised Cauliflower with Chilli (page 151)(right).

COOKING TIME:

MAKES: about ⅓ cup

60ml (4 tbsps) light soy sauce
15ml (1 tbsp) dark soy sauce
2.5ml (½ tsp) sugar
2-3 green chillies, chopped
2-3 slices fresh root ginger, minced

Mix the ingredients together and allow to stand for 10-15 minutes before using. Keep in an airtight glass jar.

Hoi Sin Sauce

PREPARATION TIME: 5 minutes

COOKING TIME: 8 minutes

MAKES: about 2 cups

This can be bought ready-made; the home-made variety does not have quite the same flavour.

15ml (1 tbsp) dark soya bean paste
2 cloves garlic, minced or very finely chopped
15ml (1 tbsp) sugar
2.5ml (½ tsp) salt
5ml (1 tsp) flour
2.5ml (½ tsp) chilli powder
450ml (¾ pint) red or white vinegar

Mix all the ingredients together in a pan and bring to the boil. Simmer gently for 5-6 minutes or until the sauce thickens. Cool and bottle.

Chilli Sauce

PREPARATION TIME: 5 minutes

COOKING TIME: 5 minutes

MAKES: about 1½ cups

25g (1oz) dried red chillies, coarsely ground
50g (2oz) dried apricots, chopped
250ml (8 fl oz) red or white vinegar
5ml (1 tsp) salt
5ml (1 tsp) sugar
5ml (1 tsp) arrowroot or cornflour

Mix all the ingredients together in a pan and bring to the boil. Simmer gently for 5 minutes until the sauce thickens. Cool and serve. Will keep bottled for a few weeks.

Lettuce and Bean Sprouts with Soy Sauce

PREPARATION TIME: 15 minutes

COOKING TIME: 5 minutes

SERVES: 4 people

100g (4oz) bean sprouts (moong or soya)
225g (8oz) sweet lettuce

This page: Pineapple Sauce. Facing page: Mixed Vegetables with Peanut Sauce.

15ml (1 tbsp) oil
2.5cm (1 inch) fresh root ginger, peeled and shredded
1 green or red chilli, seeded and split in half
Salt and freshly ground black pepper

SAUCE
30ml (2 tbsps) light soy sauce
5ml (1 tsp) dark soy sauce
10ml (2 tsps) medium white wine or rice wine
2.5ml (½ tsp) sugar
Salt and freshly ground black pepper to taste
2.5ml (½ tsp) sesame oil

Trim the bean sprouts by pinching off the grey and brown ends, as they impart a bitter taste to the dish. Pick off bean seed skin if using soya beans. Cut soya bean sprouts in 2-3 pieces. Rinse in cold water and drain. Wash and drain lettuce before shredding into 5cm (2-inch) pieces. Heat the oil in the wok and stir-fry the ginger and chilli for 1 minute. Add the lettuce and toss for 1 minute. Drain and remove to a plate. Place the bean sprouts in a colander and pour boiling water over them. Drain thoroughly and add to the lettuce. Sprinkle with salt and pepper and keep covered. Mix the sauce ingredients together in the wok. Stir over the heat until blended. Pour this sauce over the vegetables and serve immediately.

Pineapple Sauce

PREPARATION TIME: 10-15 minutes

MICROWAVE COOKING TIME: 4 minutes

MAKES: About 570ml (1 pint)

225g (8oz) can crushed pineapple, or 1 fresh pineapple, peeled and cored
7.5ml (1½ tsp) cornflour dissolved in 15ml (1 tbsp) water
15ml (1 tbsp) light soy sauce
7.5ml (1½ tsp) sugar
15ml (1 tbsp) white wine
1 piece ginger root, grated
Pinch salt

If using fresh pineapple, work in a food processor until finely chopped. Add remaining ingredients and mix well in a small, deep bowl. Cook 4 minutes on HIGH until the sauce thickens and clears. Serve with duck or prawns.

Braised Aubergine and Chicken with Chilli

PREPARATION TIME: 10 minutes

COOKING TIME: about 15 minutes

SERVES: 4 people

90ml (3 fl oz) oil
2 cloves of garlic, peeled and sliced
450g (1lb) aubergine, cut into 5x6cm (2x2½-inch) pieces
15ml (1 tbsp) soya bean paste (or canned red kidney beans, made into paste)
2.5ml (½ tsp) ground dry chilli or chilli powder
Salt
450ml (¾ pint) chicken stock
2.5cm (1-inch) fresh root ginger, peeled and sliced
2-3 spring onions, chopped
225-275g (8-10oz) chicken, shredded (cooked or uncooked)

SEASONING
30ml (2 tbsps) light soy sauce
2.5ml (½ tsp) sugar
15ml (1 tbsp) cornflour or arrowroot
30ml (2 tbsps) stock or water, if needed

Heat 60ml (4 tbsps) oil in the wok and stir-fry the garlic for 2 minutes. Add the aubergine, which will soak up all the oil. Stir-fry for 3-4 minutes, stirring constantly to avoid burning. Add the bean paste, chilli powder and salt to taste, and mix well. Add the chicken stock. Cover and cook for 4-6 minutes, simmering gently. Remove the aubergine and arrange on a dish. Save the sauce. Clean the wok and heat the remaining oil. Stir-fry the ginger for 1 minute. Add the onions and chicken and stir-fry for 2 minutes. Add the blended seasoning ingredients and the reserved aubergine sauce and simmer gently until it thickens. Pour over the aubergine and serve immediately.

Mixed Vegetables with Peanut Sauce

PREPARATION TIME: 20 minutes

COOKING TIME: 30 minutes

SERVES: 4 people as a vegetable

115g (4oz) beansprouts
115g (4oz) Chinese cabbage, shredded
115g (4oz) green beans, trimmed
Half a cucumber, cut into batons
1 carrot, peeled and cut into thin strips
1 potato, peeled and cut into thin strips
15ml (1 tbsp) peanut oil

PEANUT SAUCE
30ml (2 tbsps) peanut oil
60g (2 oz) raw shelled peanuts
2 red chillies, seeds removed, and chopped finely, or 5ml (1 tsp) chilli powder
2 shallots, peeled and chopped finely
1 clove garlic, crushed
5ml (1 tsp) brown sugar
Juice of half a lemon
100ml (3½ fl oz) coconut milk
150ml (¼ pint) water
Salt

GARNISH
Sliced hard-boiled eggs
Sliced cucumber

Heat wok and add 15ml (1 tbsp) peanut oil. When hot, toss in carrot and potato. Stir-fry for 2 minutes and add green beans and cabbage. Cook for a further 3 minutes. Add bean-sprouts and cucumber, and stir-fry for 2 minutes. Place in a serving dish. Make peanut sauce. Heat wok, add 30ml (2 tbsps) peanut oil, and fry peanuts for 2-3 minutes. Remove and drain on absorbent paper. Blend or pound chillies, shallots and garlic to a smooth paste. Grind or blend peanuts to a powder. Heat oil and fry chilli paste for 2 minutes. Add water, and bring to the boil. Add peanuts, brown sugar, lemon juice, and salt to taste. Stir until sauce is thick – about 10 minutes – and add coconut milk. Garnish vegetable dish with slices of hard-boiled egg and cucumber, and serve with peanut sauce.

Braised Cauliflower with Chilli

PREPARATION TIME: 5 minutes

COOKING TIME: 10 minutes

SERVES: 4 people

60ml (4 tbsps) oil
2.5cm (1 inch) fresh root ginger, peeled and thinly sliced
1 small cauliflower, cut into 2.5cm (1-inch) florets
2-3 green or red chillies, sliced into quarters and seeded
3 spring onions
Salt to taste
5ml (1 tsp) sugar
300ml (½ pint) chicken stock
5ml (1 tsp) cornflour or arrowroot
15ml (1 tbsp) water

Heat the wok and add the oil. Stir-fry the ginger for 1 minute. Reduce the heat and add the cauliflower and chillies. Stir-fry for 3-4 minutes. Add the spring onions, season with salt and sprinkle with sugar. Mix for 1 minute and then add the stock. Cover and cook for 2 minutes. Add the blended cornflour and water and stir over the heat until the sauce has thickened.

Bamboo Shoots with Green Vegetables

PREPARATION TIME: 10 minutes

COOKING TIME: 10-12 minutes

SERVES: 4 people

Oil for cooking
225g (8oz) spinach, or chopped broccoli

SEASONING
120ml (4 fl oz) chicken stock or water
1.25ml (¼ tsp) monosodium glutamate (optional)
1.25ml (¼ tsp) salt
1.25ml (¼ tsp) sugar
100g (4oz) bamboo shoots, sliced

SAUCE
5ml (1 tsp) light soy sauce
Pinch monosodium glutamate
5ml (1 tsp) cornflour
10ml (2 tsps) water
15ml (1 tbsp) cooked oil

Heat 30ml (2 tbsps) oil in the wok. Fry the spinach for 2 minutes and add the mixed seasoning ingredients. Simmer for 1 minute and remove from the wok onto a dish. Heat the wok and add 15ml (1 tbsp) oil. Add the bamboo shoots and fry for 1-2 minutes. Return the spinach mixture to the wok. Cook for 3 minutes. Mix together the ingredients for thickening the sauce. Add to the wok and cook for 1-2 minutes. Serve with roast Peking duck, or as a side dish.

Hot Mustard Sauce

PREPARATION TIME: 10 minutes

This page: Hot Mustard Sauce. Facing page: Stir-Fried Vegetable Medley (page 157) (top) and Sweet and Sour Cabbage (page 148) (bottom).

MICROWAVE COOKING TIME: 4 minutes

MAKES: About 200ml (6 fl oz)

60g (4 tbsps) dry mustard
60ml (4 tbsps) rice wine vinegar
7.5ml (1½ tsps) cornflour
120ml (4 fl oz) water
45ml (3 tbsps) honey
Salt

Mix together the mustard and cornflour. Beat in the water, vinegar and honey gradually until smooth. Add a small pinch of salt and cook,

uncovered, in a small, deep bowl for 4 minutes on HIGH. Stir every 30 seconds until thickened. Serve with starters or seafood.

Beans with Tree Ears and Bamboo Shoots

PREPARATION TIME: 30 minutes

MICROWAVE COOKING TIME: 4 minutes

SERVES: 4 people

6 pieces Chinese black fungi (tree or wood ears), soaked 30 minutes
340g (8 oz) French beans, cut into 5cm (2 inch) diagonal pieces
2 whole pieces canned bamboo shoots, cut into thin triangular pieces
30ml (2 tbsps) oil
30ml (2 tbsps) soy sauce
10ml (2 tsps) cornflour
60ml (4 tbsps) light stock and wine mixed
Dash sesame oil
Salt and pepper

Heat a browning dish for 5 minutes on HIGH. Pour in the oil and add the beans and bamboo shoots. Cook, uncovered, for 2 minutes on HIGH. Add the tree ears, cover the dish and leave to stand while preparing the sauce. Mix the remaining ingredients, except the sesame oil, in a glass measure. Cook for 2 minutes on HIGH, stirring once until thickened. Combine with the vegetables and stir in the sesame oil to serve.

Wok Sweet and Sour Cabbage

PREPARATION TIME: 5 minutes

COOKING TIME: 20 minutes

SERVES: 4 people as a vegetable

Half a small cabbage
30g (1oz) butter or margarine
45ml (3 tbsps) vinegar
30ml (2 tbsps) sugar
45ml (3 tbsps) water
Salt
Pepper

Slice cabbage into shreds. Melt butter in wok. Put cabbage into wok with other ingredients and set over a moderate heat. Stir until hot, then cover and simmer for 15 minutes. Adjust seasoning if necessary. Serve hot.

Spicy Cucumbers

PREPARATION TIME: 30 minutes

MICROWAVE COOKING TIME: 2 minutes

SERVES: 4 people

1 large cucumber
Salt
45ml (3 tbsps) light soy sauce
Pinch five-spice powder
1.25ml (¼ tsp) crushed red pepper
10ml (2 tsps) sesame oil
15ml (1 tbsp) rice vinegar
45ml (3 tbsps) Chinese parsley leaves

This page: Spinach, Chinese Style (page 157) (top) and Spicy Cucumbers (bottom). Facing page: Beans with Tree Ears and Bamboo Shoots.

Peel thin strips off the cucumber for a white and green stripe effect. Cut in half lengthwise, or in quarters if the cucumber is thick. Cut the lengths into 5cm (2 inch) pieces. Sprinkle with salt and leave to stand 30 minutes. Rinse and dry well. Combine the cucumber with all the remaining ingredients, except the parsley, in a deep bowl. Partially cover and cook for 2 minutes on HIGH. Add the parsley and leave in the bowl to cool. When cold, refrigerate. Serve on the same day.

Ginger Broccoli

PREPARATION TIME: 20 minutes

MICROWAVE COOKING TIME: 7-8 minutes

SERVES: 4 people

675g (1½lbs) broccoli
30ml (2 tbsps) oil
7.5cm (3-inch) piece fresh ginger root, peeled and very finely shredded
Pinch salt
Pinch sugar
5ml (1 tsp) cornflour
120ml (4 fl oz) light stock
Dash light soy sauce

Heat a browning dish for 5 minutes on HIGH. Cut off the tough ends of the broccoli stems. Cut the florets from the stems in small clusters. Peel the stems with a vegetable peeler and cut them into thin diagonal slices. Pour the oil into the browning dish and add the broccoli stem slices. Add the ginger and cook, uncovered, for 2 minutes on HIGH, stirring frequently. Add the florets, cover and set aside while preparing the sauce. Combine the remaining ingredients in a glass measure. Cook, uncovered, for 5-6 minutes on HIGH until thickened. Pour over the broccoli and stir together to serve.

Ginger Sauce

PREPARATION TIME: 5 minutes

COOKING TIME: 10 minutes

1 tbsp grated root ginger
30ml (2 tbsps) light soy sauce
15ml (1 tbsp) Chinese wine, or dry sherry
1 tsp sugar
1 tsp cornflour
30ml (2 tbsps) water
15ml (1 tbsp) oil

Heat wok, add oil and gently fry ginger. Mix together soy sauce, wine and sugar. Blend cornflour with water, and add to soy/wine mixture. Pour into wok and bring to the boil. Simmer for 3 minutes, stirring continuously. Strain through sieve. Good with seafood, pork, beef and crab rolls.

Special Fried Rice

PREPARATION TIME: 15 minutes

COOKING TIME: 20 minutes

SERVES: 4 people

2 cups boiled rice
115g (4oz) prawns or shrimp, shelled and de-veined
225g (8oz) Chinese barbecued pork, or cooked ham, diced or cut into small pieces
115g (4oz) beansprouts
115g (4oz) frozen peas
2 spring onions, sliced diagonally
15ml (1 tbsp) light soy sauce
5ml (1 tsp) dark soy sauce
30ml (2 tbsps) peanut oil
Salt
Pepper

PANCAKE
2 eggs, beaten

Salt

GARNISH

2 spring onion flowers (trim spring onions, slice lengthways, leaving one end intact and leave in cold water in refrigerator until curling).

Heat wok and add 15ml (1 tbsp) peanut oil. Roll oil around surface. Make pancake by mixing beaten eggs with a pinch of salt and 5ml (1 tsp) oil. Add egg mixture to wok, and move wok back and forth so that the mixture spreads over the surface. When lightly browned on the underside, turn over and cook on other side. Set aside to cool. Heat remaining oil in wok. When hot, add spring onions and peas and cook, covered, for 2 minutes. With a slotted spoon, remove and set aside. Re-heat oil and add rice. Stir continuously over a low heat until rice is heated through. Add soy sauces and mix well. Add peas, spring onions, bean-sprouts, meat, prawns, and salt and pepper to taste. Mix thoroughly. Serve hot, garnished with pancake and spring onion flowers. The pancake may be sliced very finely and mixed in if desired.

Spinach, Chinese Style

PREPARATION TIME: 15 minutes

MICROWAVE COOKING TIME: 2 minutes plus 1 minute standing time

SERVES: 4 people

675g (1½lbs) fresh spinach, stalks removed
30ml (2 tbsps) oil
Salt
Sugar
Soy sauce
2 spring onions, white part only, finely sliced

Wash the spinach well and pat the leaves dry. Heat a browning dish for 4 minutes on HIGH. Pour in the oil and add the spinach. Add a pinch of salt and sugar and cook, uncovered, for 2 minutes on HIGH, stirring frequently. Add the spring onions and a dash of soy sauce. Leave to stand 1 minute before serving.

Stir-Fried Vegetable Medley

PREPARATION TIME: 20 minutes

COOKING TIME: 10 minutes

SERVES: 4 people as a vegetable

2 carrots, cut into flowers (slice strips out lengthways to produce flowers when cut across into rounds)
1 can baby sweetcorn, drained

Facing page: Ginger Broccoli. This page: Special Fried Rice (top) and Ginger Sauce (bottom).

2 cups broccoli florets (slit stems to ensure quick cooking)
1 onion, peeled and sliced in julienne strips
2 sticks celery, with tough strings removed, sliced diagonally in half-moon shapes
1 courgette, sliced diagonally
1 clove garlic, crushed
15ml (1 tbsp) light soy sauce
1.25ml (¼ tsp) finely-grated ginger
30ml (2 tbsps) oil
Salt
Pepper

Prepare all ingredients in advance. Heat wok and add oil. Add ginger, garlic, onion, carrots, broccoli and courgette, and toss in oil for 2-3 minutes. Add celery and baby sweetcorn, and toss 1-2 minutes longer. Season with soy sauce, and salt and pepper if desired. Add cornflour to thicken vegetable juices if necessary.

This page: Yang Chow Fried Rice (top right) and Plain Fried Rice (page 43) (bottom left). Facing page: Ten Varieties of Beauty (page 160).

Yang Chow Fried Rice

PREPARATION TIME: 10 minutes

COOKING TIME: 6-8 minutes

SERVES: 6 people

45ml (3 tbsps) cooking oil
1 egg, beaten
100g (4oz) cooked meat, chopped (pork, lamb, beef)
100g (4oz) cooked prawns or shrimp, shelled and chopped
50g (2oz) shelled green peas
2 spring onions, chopped

450g (1lb) dry, cooked rice
Salt to taste
5ml (1 tsp) monosodium glutamate (optional)

Heat 15ml (1 tbsp) oil in a wok. Fry the beaten egg until set, and break into small lumps. Remove the egg. Add the remaining oil and fry the meat, prawns, peas and onions for 1-2 minutes. Add the cooked rice and sprinkle with salt and monosodium glutamate. Fry for 3 minutes. Mix in the cooked egg and serve immediately.

Mango Sauce

PREPARATION TIME: 5 minutes

COOKING TIME: 20 minutes

SERVES:

1 can sliced mangoes
150ml (¼ pint) malt vinegar
2.5ml (½ tsp) garam masala
5ml (1 tsp) grated root ginger
15ml (1 tbsp) sugar
5ml (1 tsp) oil
Salt

Heat wok and add oil. Add garam masala and ginger, and cook for 1 minute. Add undrained mangoes, vinegar, sugar, and salt to taste. Simmer, uncovered, for 15 minutes. Blend and push through a sieve. Good with chicken, beef and spring rolls.

Ten Varieties of Beauty

PREPARATION TIME: 20 minutes

MICROWAVE COOKING TIME: 6-8 minutes

SERVES: 4-6 people

60ml (4 tbsps) oil
3 sticks celery, diagonally sliced
2 carrots, peeled and cut into ribbons with a vegetable peeler
90g (3oz) mangetout
1 red pepper, thickly sliced
4 spring onions, diagonally sliced
8 ears of baby corn
60g (2oz) bean sprouts
10 water chestnuts, sliced
½ small can sliced bamboo shoots
10 Chinese dried mushrooms, soaked in hot water, stalks removed
280ml (½ pint) chicken stock
30ml (2 tbsps) cornflour
45ml (3 tbsps) light soy sauce
Sesame oil

Heat a browning dish for 5 minutes on HIGH. Pour in the oil and add the celery and carrots. Cook for 1 minute on HIGH. Remove from the dish and add the mangetout, red pepper and corn. Cook for 1 minute on HIGH and place with the celery and carrots. Add the onions, bean sprouts, water chestnuts and bamboo shoots to the dish. Cook for 1 minute on HIGH, adding the mushrooms after 30 seconds. Place with the rest of vegetables. Combine the remaining ingredients in a glass measure. Cook 2-3 minutes on HIGH until thickened. Taste and add salt if necessary. Pour over the vegetables and stir carefully. Reheat for 1-2 minutes on HIGH before serving.

Julienne of Vegetables

PREPARATION TIME: 20 minutes

COOKING TIME: 15 minutes

SERVES: 4 people as a vegetable

2 medium onions, peeled and cut into matchstick strips
2 carrots, scraped and cut into matchstick strips
1 parsnip, scraped and cut into matchstick strips
2 sticks celery, cut into matchstick strips
1 turnip, peeled and cut into matchstick strips
15ml (1 tbsp) oil
30ml (2 tbsps) water
15g (½oz) butter
Salt
Pepper

Prepare vegetables. Heat wok and add oil. Stir-fry vegetable strips over gentle heat for 5 minutes. Add water and salt to taste, and increase heat. Cook for a further 5 minutes over high heat. Drain any liquid from wok. Add butter and freshly-ground black pepper, and toss to coat well.

Sweet and Sour Sauce

PREPARATION TIME: 10 minutes

COOKING TIME: 10 minutes

SERVES:

Juice of 2 oranges
30ml (2 tbsps) lemon juice
30ml (2 tbsps) white wine vinegar
15ml (1 tbsp) sugar
15ml (1 tbsp) tomato purée
15ml (1 tbsp) light soy sauce
2.5ml (½ tsp) salt
15ml (1 tbsp) cornflour
30ml (2 tbsps) water
Pinch of red food colouring, if desired

Combine orange and lemon juice, sugar, vinegar, tomato purée, soy sauce, salt, and red colouring, if using. Place in wok and heat gently. Blend cornflour with water, and stir into sauce. Bring to boil and simmer for 3 minutes, stirring continuously. Good with fish, pork, wontons and spring rolls.

Ratatouille

PREPARATION TIME: 30 minutes

COOKING TIME: 30 minutes

SERVES: 4 people as a vegetable

1 aubergine, sliced into 2.5cm (1-inch) slices
2 courgettes, sliced diagonally
4 tomatoes, chopped roughly
2 onions, peeled and quartered
1 red pepper, cored, seeds removed, and chopped roughly
1 green pepper, cored, seeds removed, and chopped roughly
3 cloves garlic, crushed
5ml (1 tsp) dry basil
60ml (4 tbsps) olive oil
Salt
Pepper

Slice aubergine and sprinkle with salt. Leave for 20 minutes. Rinse in water, and dry on absorbent paper. Chop roughly. Heat wok and add oil. Add onions, garlic and basil. Cover and cook gently until onion is soft but not coloured. Add peppers, courgettes and aubergine. Cover and fry gently for 15 minutes, stirring occasionally. Add

tomatoes and salt and pepper to taste and cook, covered, for a further 10 minutes. Serve hot or chilled.

Fried Bean Curd with Mushrooms

PREPARATION TIME: 15 minutes

COOKING TIME: 12-15 minutes

SERVES: 4 people

225g (8oz) large cap mushrooms, sliced

SEASONING

15ml (1 tbsp) rice wine or dry sherry
10ml (2 tsps) sugar
4 dried Chinese mushrooms, soaked and sliced

Above: Okra and Tomatoes.

Pinch bicarbonate of soda
225g (8oz) mustard green or spinach, cut into 7.5cm (3-inch) pieces
4 squares bean curd (tofu), cubed
Oil
2.5cm (1 inch) fresh root ginger, peeled and shredded
2 spring onions, chopped
50g (2oz) cooked ham, shredded

SAUCE

15ml (1 tbsp) oyster sauce
5ml (1 tsp) dark soy sauce
15ml (1 tbsp) cornflour
60ml (4 tbsps) stock or water
Freshly ground black pepper

Blanch the fresh mushrooms in water for 1 minute. Drain the mushrooms and discard the water. Mix the seasoning ingredients together and marinate the mushrooms for 5-6 minutes. Discard marinade. Bring 1.2 litres (2 pints) of water to the boil and add the bicarbonate of soda and salt. Blanch the greens for 2 minutes. Drain the greens. Discard water. Sprinkle 2.5ml (½ tsp) salt over the bean curd. Deep-fry in hot oil until golden brown. Drain and remove. Heat 30ml (2 tbsps) oil in the wok and stir-fry the ginger, onions and ham for 2-3 minutes. Return the mushrooms to the wok and mix with the ginger and onions. Add the blended sauce ingredients and bring to boil. Add the bean curd and simmer until the sauce thickens. Arrange the greens on a dish and pour the sauce over them. Sprinkle with freshly ground black pepper.

Okra and Tomatoes

PREPARATION TIME: 15 minutes

COOKING TIME: 10 minutes

SERVES: 4 people as a vegetable

225g (8oz) okra , sliced into 1.5cm (½-inch) pieces
1 onion, peeled and chopped
2 tomatoes, chopped
1 red chilli, seeds removed, and sliced finely
1.25 ml (¼ tsp) turmeric
1.25 ml (¼ tsp) chilli powder
2.5ml (½ tsp) garam masala
15ml (1 tbsp) oil or ghee
150ml (¼ pint) water
Salt

Heat wok and add oil or ghee. When hot, add turmeric, chilli powder and garam masala, and fry for 30 seconds. Add onion, okra and red chilli, and stir-fry for 3 minutes. Add tomatoes, water, and salt to taste, and cook, uncovered, for 5 minutes or until sauce thickens.

Fried Vegetables with Ginger

PREPARATION TIME: 10 minutes

COOKING TIME: 13-15 minutes

Inset Left: Fried Vegetables with Ginger (page 161) (top right) and Fried Bean Curd with Mushrooms (page 161) (bottom). Ratatouille (page 160) (right) and Julienne of Vegetables (page 160) (bottom right).

SERVES: 6 people

1kg (2¼lb) mixed Chinese green vegetables (cabbage, spinach, kale, broccoli, Chinese leaf etc.)
50g (2oz) mangetout
5ml (1 tsp) bicarbonate of soda
10ml (2 tsp) sugar
5ml (1 tsp) salt
15ml (1 tbsp) cooked oil
45ml (3 tbsps) oil
2.5cm (1 inch) fresh root ginger, peeled and shredded
1 green pepper, seeded and diced
1 green or red chilli, sliced into strips

SAUCE
10ml (2 tsps) dark soy sauce
5ml (1 tsp) sugar
250ml (8 fl oz) chicken stock
10ml (2 tsps) cornflour
5ml (1 tsp) five spice powder

TO SERVE
2.5ml (½ tsp) sesame oil
Freshly ground black pepper to taste

Cut greens into 7.5cm (3-inch) pieces. Bring a large pan of water to the boil and add the seasoning ingredients. Add the mangetout and greens and cook for 4-5 minutes. Drain green vegetables and discard water. Add 15ml (1 tbsp) oil to the vegetables and keep covered. Heat the remaining oil in the wok and stir-fry the ginger for 1 minute. Add the green pepper and chillies and stir-fry for 1-2 minutes. Add the blended sauce ingredients and stir well. Simmer gently for 3-4 minutes. Add the green vegetables and cook for 1 minute. Serve immediately, sprinkled with sesame oil and pepper.

Chinese COOKING

DESSERTS

Almond Cookies

PREPARATION TIME: 20 minutes

COOKING TIME: 12-15 minutes

MAKES: 60 cookies

225g (8oz) lard
100g (4oz) caster sugar
50g (2oz) brown sugar
1 egg, beaten
Few drops almond essence
275g (10oz) plain flour
Pinch salt
7.5ml (1½ tsp) baking powder
75g (3oz) blanched almonds
1 egg yolk
30ml (2 tbsps) water

Cream the lard with the caster sugar and the brown sugar until light and fluffy. Add the egg and almond essence and beat until smooth. Sift the flour, salt and baking powder. Mix the dry ingredients into the creamed mixture. Shape into small balls on a lightly floured surface. Flatten slightly and press an almond into the centre of each one. Place onto a greased baking sheet. Mix the egg yolk with the water. Brush the cookies with the egg glaze. Bake at 180°C, 350°F, Gas Mark 4, for 12-15 minutes.

Sweet Dumplings

PREPARATION TIME: 10 minutes

COOKING TIME: 15-20 minutes

MAKES: 10-12

Oil
75g (3oz) sugar
100g (4oz) plain red bean paste
50g (2oz) desiccated coconut
4 egg whites
15ml (1 tbsp) plain flour
45ml (3 tbsps) cornflour
Icing sugar

Heat 15ml (1 tbsp) oil in a wok and add the sugar, bean paste and coconut. Stir-fry for 4-5 minutes until the sugar melts and the paste is smooth and shiny. Fry for a few minutes more and then allow to cool on a dish. Whisk the egg whites until stiff and mix with the plain flour and cornflour to a smooth batter. Beat well. Clean the wok and heat sufficient oil for deep frying. Make 10-12 even-sized balls from the bean paste mixture. Dip each ball into the batter and then deep-fry for 3-4 minutes, until golden and crisp. Fry a few at a time and drain on kitchen paper. Dust with icing sugar before serving.

Steamed Custard

PREPARATION TIME: 10 minutes

COOKING TIME: 20 minutes

SERVES:

450ml (¾ pint) milk
30g (1oz) sugar
2 eggs, beaten
3 drops vanilla essence
Sprinkling of ground nutmeg or cinnamon

Place sugar and milk in wok. Heat gently until the milk reaches a low simmer and the sugar has dissolved. Remove from wok and leave to cool for 5 minutes. Meanwhile, wash wok and place steaming rack inside, with 4-5cm (1½-2 inches) of hot water. Return to heat and bring water to simmering point. Pour milk and sugar mixture over beaten eggs. Beat again, and add the vanilla essence, stirring well. Pour mixture into a heat-proof dish or metal moulds and sprinkle lightly with nutmeg or cinnamon. Place on rack and cover with greaseproof paper, so condensation does not drop into custard. Cover wok and steam for 10-15 minutes. When cooked, a knife inserted in centre will come out clean, and custard will be set and gelatinous. Cover and cool for 1 hour, then place in refrigerator until needed.

Bananas Cooked in Coconut Milk

PREPARATION TIME: 20 minutes

COOKING TIME: 20 minutes

SERVES: 4 people

4-6 large, ripe bananas, peeled and sliced diagonally into 3 or 4 pieces
15ml (1 tbsp) brown sugar
115g (4oz) desiccated coconut
450ml (¾ pint) milk

GARNISH
Desiccated coconut

Put sugar, coconut and milk into wok, and bring to simmering point. Turn off heat and allow to cool for 15 minutes. Push through sieve or a piece of muslin to squeeze out juices. Return to wok, and simmer for 10 minutes, or until creamy. Add bananas, and cook slowly until bananas are soft. Serve immediately sprinkled with desiccated coconut.

Facing page: Sweet Dumplings (top) and Almond Cookies (centre left).

Red Bean Filled Dim Sums

PREPARATION TIME: 45-50 minutes

COOKING TIME: 10-12 minutes

MAKES: about 24

50g (2oz) sugar
300ml (½ pint) warm water
15ml (1 tbsp) dried yeast
450g (1lb) plain flour
30ml (2 tbsps) melted lard
1 egg white, beaten

FILLING
275g (10oz) sweet bean paste, ready made
Red food colouring

Dissolve the sugar in the warm water and add the yeast. Stir until dissolved. Leave in a warm place until frothy. Sift the flour into a mixing bowl and add the melted lard and the yeast mixture. Mix together. Turn the mixture onto a floured surface and knead to a smooth and elastic dough. Roll into a long sausage and divide into 24 equal portions. Roll each portion into a 5cm (2-inch) flat circle. Brush edges of dough with beaten egg white. Place 15ml (1 tbsp) of filling into the centre of each circle and pull the dough around it to enclose the filling. Pleat the open edges in a circular fashion, so that a small opening is left in the middle of the pleating. Place a small piece of greased foil over the pleats on each dim sum. Leave for 10-12 minutes until the dough becomes springy to the touch. Put a dab of red food colouring on each dim sum. Arrange the dim sums in a bamboo steaming basket and steam over boiling water for 10-12 minutes. The dim sums are ready when they are dry and smooth. Alternatively they can be baked at 180°C, 350°F, Gas Mark 4, for about 20 minutes.

Chinese Bean Buns

PREPARATION TIME: about 2 hours, including proving time

COOKING TIME: about 30 minutes

MAKES: about 14

60ml (2 fl oz) milk
50g (2 oz) sugar
2.5ml (½ tsp) salt
25g (1oz) lard
60ml (2 fl oz) warm water
10ml (2 tsps) dried yeast
1 egg, beaten
275g (10oz) plain flour

FILLING
100g (4oz) sweet bean paste
25g (1oz) sugar
25g (1oz) chopped walnuts
15ml (1 tbsp) lard

Bring the milk almost to the boil. Stir in the sugar, salt and lard. Cool slightly. Put the warm water and yeast into a bowl and stir to mix. Add the lukewarm milk mixture. Add the beaten egg and 225g (8oz) of the flour and beat until smooth. Add the remaining flour and mix to a dough. Turn dough out onto a well-floured board and knead until smooth and elastic. Place in a greased bowl. Brush the dough with oil and cover. Leave to rise in a warm place until doubled in size (about 1 hour).
Heat the filling ingredients together in a wok for 5-6 minutes until smooth and shiny. Remove and cool. Divide the filling into 12-14 portions. Knead the risen dough again for 2 minutes and then divide the dough into 12-14 portions. Flatten into thick, circular shapes 10cm (4 inches) in diameter. Place a chopstick on each circle of dough to mark it in half, and then in half again. Cut along the marks to within ⅓ of the centre. Place one portion of filling in the centre of the dough circle and fold the cut ends in to meet in the centre to form a rosette. Secure by pinching ends of dough together. Place a piece of greased foil over the pinched ends and place the buns on a greased baking tray. Brush with a little milk. Bake at 190°C, 375°F, Gas Mark 5 for 20-25 minutes.

This page: Chinese Bean Buns (top left) and Red Bean Filled Dim Sums (right). Facing page: Steamed Custard (page 164) (top) and Bananas Cooked in Coconut Milk (page 164) (bottom).

Jade Pieces

PREPARATION TIME: 1 hour

MICROWAVE COOKING TIME: 43-49 minutes

MAKES: 24 pieces (approx)

450g (1lb) green split peas, soaked overnight, or brought to the boil, cooked 10 minutes on HIGH and left to stand for 1 hour
120g (4oz) sugar
850ml (1½ pints) water
60ml (4 tbsps) cornflour
1 piece preserved ginger, finely chopped
45ml (3 tbsps) desiccated coconut
Few drops green food colouring

Drain the peas and return them to a large glass bowl. Add the water, loosely cover the bowl and cook on HIGH for 40-45 minutes, or until the peas are very soft. Purée the peas with the sugar and food colouring. Mix the cornflour with a little water and add to the peas. Return to the bowl and cook, uncovered, 3-4 minutes until cornflour thickens. Add the ginger and pour into a shallow dish to the depth of 2.5cm (1 inch). Sprinkle the coconut over the surface and chill until firm. Cut into diamond shapes to serve.

Stuffed Lychees

PREPARATION TIME: 20 minutes

COOKING TIME:

SERVES:

450g (1lb) canned lychees, stones removed
225g (8oz) canned pineapple rings
Few drops vanilla essence or almond essence

Drain the lychees into a bowl, reserving the juice. Drain the pineapple rings and reserve the liquid. Slice each pineapple ring into 2.5cm (1-inch) long strips. Press one or two strips of pineapple into each lychee. Arrange the pineapple-filled lychees in a deep serving dish. Mix the pineapple and lychee liquid with a few drops of essence. Spoon over the stuffed fruits. Serve well chilled. Alternatively, stuff the lychees with maraschino cherries, mango, canned pears, oranges etc.

Sweet Almond Pudding

PREPARATION TIME: 4-5 minutes

COOKING TIME: 6 minutes

SERVES: 4-6 people

175g (6oz) blanched almonds
450ml (¾ pint) water
175g (6oz) sugar
45ml (3 tbsps) rice powder, or ground rice
150ml (¼ pint) milk

Blend the blanched almonds and water in the liquidiser. Put into a pan and bring to the boil. Add the sugar and stir over the heat until the sugar has dissolved. Add the rice slowly to the milk and stir gradually over the simmering sugar and almond mixture. Cook gently until the mixture thickens. Remove from the heat and pour into a serving dish. Serve hot or cold.

Agar-Agar Pudding

PREPARATION TIME: 5 minutes

COOKING TIME: 4-5 minutes

SERVES: 4 people

600ml (1 pint) milk
100g (4oz) sugar
25g (1oz) ground almonds
50g (2oz) agar-agar
25g (1oz) almonds, blanched and chopped

Mix the milk, sugar and ground almonds together in a pan and stir over the heat for 4 minutes. Add the agar-agar and stir until dissolved. Stir in the chopped almonds. Pour into a shallow dish 2.5cm (1 inch) deep. Cool and keep in refrigerator until set. Serve chilled, cut into diamond or square shapes.

Date and Red Bean Winter Pudding

PREPARATION TIME: 20 minutes

MICROWAVE COOKING TIME: 17-22 minutes plus 3 minutes standing time

SERVES: 4 people

450g (1lb) dried, stoned dates
850ml (1½ pints) water
180g (6oz) red bean paste
225g (½lb) sugar
60ml (4 tbsps) cornflour
90g (3oz) white vegetable shortening or margarine
Pinch salt
2.5ml (½ tsp) almond essence
30ml (2 tbsps) sliced almonds

Place the dates in a large bowl and add the water. Cover loosely and cook 12-16 minutes on HIGH, or until the water boils and the dates begin to soften. Leave to stand 3 minutes. Drain the water from the dates, reserve 570ml (1 pint) of the liquid to mix with the cornflour, and cook 3-4 minutes on HIGH to thicken. Combine the dates, sugar, bean paste, shortening or margarine, salt and almond essence in a food processor and purée until smooth. Mix into the thickened date liquid and cook for 2 minutes on HIGH, stirring frequently. Pour into a serving bowl and chill. Sprinkle with almonds. May be served with cream if desired.

Facing page: Date and Red Bean Winter Pudding (top) (and) and Jade Pieces (bottom). This page: Stuffed Lychees (left), Sweet Almond Pudding (centre) and Agar-Agar Pudding (right).

Chinese COOKING

GLOSSARY

Agar-Agar This is a specially-prepared, dried seaweed which is sold in the shops as Chinese grass. The white, fibrous strands require soaking and are used like gelatine. Agar-agar is also sold in powder form. It is used for puddings and as a setting agent. All Chinese and Oriental food shops should sell it.

Arrowroot The starch extract of the ground root of an American plant, used as a thickening agent for sauces.

Bean Curd This come in soft, custard-like squares and is made from soy beans. It is highly nutritious and is one of the most important Chinese foods. It is available only from Chinese grocers and is also sold in dried form as bean curd stick, in brine, and fried.

Bean Pastes Sauces made from soy beans which are sold in cans and jars. Once opened, they should be kept refrigerated. There are many varieties of bean paste:
Hot Bean Paste is made with chillies and is salty.
Soy Bean Paste is dark in colour, very salty and is made with fermented soy beans.
Sweet Bean Paste is made with black soy beans, sugar, flour and spices.
Yellow Bean Paste is made with yellow soy beans and is also quite salty in taste.

Bean Sprouts These are the shoots of mung beans or soy beans. Soy beans are stronger in flavour. They are readily available from most supermarkets and Oriental shops. Fresh bean sprouts will keep for several days if refrigerated in a perforated plastic bag; discard any discoloured shoots. The topped and tailed sprouts are known as 'Silver Sprouts' and are used for very special dishes.

Black Bean Sauce This can be bought ready-made from shops, or made with 3-4 tbsps steamed, black soy beans mixed to a paste with 2 tbsps oil and 2 tbsps sugar.

Chilli Oil This can be brought ready-prepared. Chilli oil can also be made by infusing dried chillies in hot vegetable oil, although it will not keep for as long as the ready-prepared variety.

Chilli Peppers There are numerous varieties of chilli peppers, varying in size and strength of flavour. Commonly used in eastern cooking are the red and green finger-like chilli peppers, about 4 inches long, and the tiny red and green birds-eye chilli peppers, which are very hot. When preparing chilli peppers, it is advisable to wear rubber gloves and avoid getting the oils near the lips and eyes. The seeds, which are very hot, should be discard unless a very fiery dish is desired.

Chilli Powder Dried fruit pod of the capsicum plant, in flaked or powdered form. It is very hot and spicy, and should be purchased only in small quantities.

Chilli Sauce This is a very hot, spicy and tangy sauce made from chillies and vinegar. Chilli sauce can be purchased from many supermarkets and all Chinese grocers. It is used to season a wide variety of savoury Chinese dishes.

Chinese Broccoli A dark green, leafy vegetable which bears small white flowers; it looks very much like miniature broccoli. It is sold only in Chinese grocers and, if not available, can be substituted by Chinese leaves or ordinary broccoli.

Chinese Dates These are sold in dried form and will keep for a month. There are two varieties: black and red, and they can be purchased from most Oriental shops. They resemble dried prunes and are used in sweet and some savoury, stir-fried dishes. Ordinary dried dates can easily be used in their place.

Chinese Leaves There are two main varieties. One is called Pak-choy, and the other, a more tender flowering white cabbage, is called Choy-sum. Chinese leaves and Tiensin cabbage are sold in supermarkets and Oriental shops, and also in many fruit and vegetable markets. Chinese leaves are tightly packed and have creamy white leaves with a thick central stalk. They are often used in salads in place of lettuce. All these cabbages can be substituted by ordinary cabbage.

Chinese Parsley Otherwise known as fresh coriander, this is a herb of Indian origin which is used as a flavouring and a garnish. The flat leaves have a strong flavour and cannot be substituted by Western parsley.

Chinese Wine There are many kinds of wine made from rice. Chinese rice wine can be substituted by ordinary dry sherry in most recipes. Rice wines vary considerably in quality, but they are all very strong.

Chives Now available in most parts of the world, these have a subtle onion taste and bright green stems which are used as a garnish for soups and other dishes.

Cinnamon Delicate, sweet spice which is the dried, aromatic bark of a type of laurel. Cinnamon can be purchased in bark, quill or powdered form.

Cloud Ear This is known by many names i.e. wood ear, snow fungus, sea jelly or jelly sheet. It is actually a dried fungus which, when soaked in water, resembles a puffed ear, hence the name. It has no flavour and is used only to add texture to a dish. It will keep for about a month in its dried form.

Cloves The dried, aromatic buds of a type or myrtle native to Southeast Asia. Used whole, or with the central bud ground into a powder, cloves have preserving properties, and are used in both sweet and savoury dishes.

Cooked Oil Many Chinese dishes require the use of cooked oil. It is made by heating vegetable, peanut or any other kind of oil until it smokes.

Cornflour A fine, white maize flour used as a thickener, mainly for sauces.

Fennel (dried) This is sold in seed form and the tiny, pale green seeds resemble caraway seeds. Fennel is sold in supermarkets, health food shops and in Chinese grocery shops, and it is an important ingredient in five spice powder.

Five Spice Powder This is a strong, coffee-coloured seasoning made with equal parts of finely-ground fagara (brown peppercorns), cinnamon bark, clove, fennel and star anise. Use sparingly.

Flour Many varieties of flour are used in Chinese cookery, the main one being the ordinary plain type, which is usually a finely ground wheat flour. It is used to make most steamed breads and some pastries.
High Gluten Flour this is used to make wonton wrappers. It is a strong flour with a high gluten content and can therefore be rolled very thinly.
Tang Flour This is made from a low-gluten wheat. The flour is used for making clear wrappers for Dim Sum because, when cooked, this flour becomes transparent.

Ginger Fresh root ginger is a vital ingredient in Chinese cooking; nearly all the traditional meat and fish dishes use root ginger. Sprouting ginger is the best and it is used for preserving foods in vinegar and for pickling. The tough, older roots are strong in flavour. The texture may be fibrous, but if you chop the ginger finely with a sharp knife it will release its full flavour. Ginger not only gives a distinct taste to a dish but it helps the digestion as well. Fresh ginger cannot be substituted by ground or preserved ginger. It is widely available.

Glutinous Rice This is also known as 'sticky' rice. It is a special variety of Chinese rice which has opaque grains, and when cooked turns transparent and very sticky. It is used for making both desserts and savoury dishes.

Hoisin Sauce This is a sweet, brownish-red sauce made from soy beans, salt, sugar, chilli, garlic, vinegar and flour. It has a sweet, tangy flavour and can be bought from Chinese shops or large supermarkets. It is used in cooking as well as being served as a dip for meats etc. It is also known as seafood sauce or barbecue sauce.

Long Beans These are one of the many typical Chinese vegetables. As the name suggests, they are longer than ordinary beans. They are obtainable from most Chinese shops and from Oriental grocers and can be substituted by lobia beans or ordinary green beans.

Lotus Root is available canned or fresh from Chinese groceries. Cut in thin rounds, it has a flower-like appearance. Obtained from waterlilies. Seeds are available preserved or fresh at Chinese New Year and reputedly bring good luck. Leaves are available from Chinese groceries to cook in or on. Should be soaked first.

Monosodium Glutamate This is a white, crystalline substance commonly known as MSG. It is used extensively in Chinese cookery for tenderising meat and for enhancing the flavour of dishes. It is sometimes sold under the names of Aji No Moto and Vi Tsin and is also called 'taste powder'. It should be used sparingly, as too much will spoil the dish, and can be totally omitted from recipes if preferred.

Mooli Mooli or muli is a crisp, white variety of radish. It grows to about 25cm/10 inches in length and 10cm/4 inches in diameter. It has a stronger taste than ordinary red radish and is eaten in salads and as a vegetable. It has a crunchy texture and a sharp flavour.

Mushrooms There are many varieties of dried mushrooms which are used in Chinese cooking. Follow the recipe to see the type suggested. To prepare dried mushrooms for cooking, soak in hot water for ½ hour. Drain and season with ½ tbsp wine and little sugar. (See also Chinese Mushrooms and Cloud Ear.)

Mustard Green This is also known as leaf mustard. It has a slightly bitter taste and is crunchy in texture. It is used in soups and stir-fried dishes. It is only sold in Oriental and Chinese grocery shops. Use broccoli as the nearest substitute.

Noodles There are many different kinds of noodles. Some are made from wheat flour, some from rice flour and some from bean flour. All these varieties of noodles are obtainable from Chinese and Oriental grocers, and many are sold in supermarkets and other food shops. Noodles can be substituted by spaghetti, though the flavour will not be the same.
Bean Thread Noodles Thin, white, transparent noodles made from moong bean flour. They should be soaked before use.
Cake Noodles These are bound together in tight balls.
Rice Sheet Noodles These are made from rice and come in wide, flat sheets. They are also sold in dried form.
Rice Stick Noodles Sometimes called rice vermicelli, these are very thin noodles made from rice. They must be soaked in hot water for 10-12 minutes before use. If deep-fried they become very light and crisp, like wafers.
Shanghai Noodles, Thin These are mostly used in soups and are thin and

pale in color. The basic noodles are made from wheat flour.
Shanghai Noodles, Thick These are yellowish in colour and are made from wheat flour enriched with egg. Commonly sold in fried form in the shape of small and large cakes, they are also sold fresh in Chinese shops. Fresh noodles can be kept in plastic bags in the refrigerator for up to 1 week.

Oyster Sauce This is a special sauce produced from soy sauce and oysters which have been fermented together. It is used as a flavouring, colouring and also as a condiment. Once opened it will keep in the bottle for several months.

Preserved Chinese Vegetables These are specially prepared dried vegetables which retain their original flavour. Preserved vegetables are also sold in cans and jars, packed in a brine solution.

Rice There are many different varieties of rice. Long grained rice is the variety usually used for making simple rice dishes, but a special, glutinous, medium-grain rice is used for making desserts and savoury dishes.

Sesame Oil An aromatic oil produced from sesame seeds. This has a special flavour and is used both as a seasoning and as a vital ingredient in some sauces. Sold in bottles, it is available from most general grocery and healthfood shops.

Snow Peas Also known as pea pods and mangetout, these are delicate, flat pea pods. The whole vegetable is eaten. They are either eaten raw or lightly cooked, and they add character and colour to many dishes. Will keep for a few days if kept in perforated plastic bags in the refrigerator.

Soy Sauce There are two kinds of soy sauce: one is dark and the other is light. Made from fermented soy beans, both varieties are used for flavouring soups, stir-fried dishes and for seasoning nearly all Chinese foods. The dark soy sauce is thicker and stronger in flavour, while the lighter varieties are the weaker infusions of the fermented beans. The first extract is the strongest and the best. Soy sauces are sometimes flavoured with mushrooms, oysters and shrimp roe.

Star Anise This is an eight-pointed clove with a strong anise smell and flavour, and is one of the spices which goes into Chinese five spice powder. It can be purchased in powder or whole form. It is used to flavour red-cooked poultry and many meat dishes.

Stocks Chinese cooking needs stock of one sort or another in almost all dishes. There are two main kinds of stock that are used. It is very useful to make home-made stock, which will keep refrigerated for 5-7 days. Alternatively, stock cubes can be substituted.

Chicken Stock 2lbs chicken trimmings (bones, neck, skin, wings etc), 2 litres/ 3½ pints water, 1 inch fresh root ginger, peeled and chopped, 1 medium onion, peeled and thinly sliced, salt, freshly ground black pepper. Put chicken trimmings and water into a pan. Bring to the boil and simmer for 10 minutes. Skim and add ginger, onions and seasoning; simmer for 1-1½ hours. Strain and use.

Superior Stock or Strong Stock 1 boiling chicken, 100g/4oz loin of pork, cubed, 25g/1oz Yunnan ham, cubed, 2 litres/ 3½ pints water, 1cm/½ inch fresh root ginger, peeled and thinly sliced, 2 spring onions, chopped, salt, freshly ground black pepper. Place chicken, pork and ham into a pan with the water and bring to the boil. Cook for 10 minutes and skim. Add ginger and spring onions and season with salt and pepper. Simmer for 1½ hours. The fat should not be skimmed off completely as this gives the stock its characteristic flavour.

Tangerine Peel, Dried The best sun-dried peels are several years old. Peel is used as a seasoning for stews and other dishes. It is a little expensive, however, and can be omitted from the recipe, or substituted by home-dried peels.

Vinegar Chinese vinegars are made from fermented rice by the process of distillation, and there are four main varieties:
Black Vinegar This is similar to malt vinegar, but not quite as strong. It has a stronger flavour than other Chinese varieties, and is used both as a flavouring and as a condiment.
Red Vinegar This is distinctly red in colour as the name suggests, and is used particularly with seafood dishes and as a condiment.
Sweet Vinegar This is almost like port in flavour, very sweet and rich black in colour. It is used mainly for braised and stewed dishes and has a sharp taste.
White Vinegar This is not as strong as European white vinegar; it is milder and more tangy. When substituting one vinegar for another, taste carefully.

Water Chestnuts These are the bulb-like stems of the bulrush. They are slightly sweet and have a crisp texture. They are usually sold in cans; occasionally they are sold in their natural form. They are available from some supermarkets and all Oriental and Chinese shops. Canned water chestnuts will keep for 3-4 weeks after opening if refrigerated and kept in water. The water should be changed daily. Chestnuts are also ground to a flour which is used for making batter.

Winter Melon This is a very large, green-skinned melon with a soft, white flesh and a delicate taste. It is sold fresh in Chinese shops or Oriental grocers, but can also be purchased cubed in cans. Peeled and seeded marrow or cucumber can be used as a substitute.

Wonton Wrappers or Skins Very thin wrappers made from a mixture of wheat, eggs and water. These can be purchased ready-made, usually in 7.5cm /3-inch squares, or made at home.

Worcestershire Sauce A hot sauce containing malt vinegar, molasses, chilli peppers, spices, anchovies and tropical fruits. It should be used sparingly.

Yunnan Ham This is a special kind of Chinese smoked ham which is produced by a salting and smoking process. Substitute: good cuts of European smoked ham, smoked gammon or lean rashers of smoked bacon.

Chinese COOKING INDEX